Polumbus Library
of
Youth Soccer
Coaching Books
Book III

PRACTICE SESSIONS

With Commentaries ™

Ages 5-8

By
R.T. Polumbus

Cover Design: Lindsay Polumbus

Layout & Design: Pete Wilkins

Illustrations: Jim Jensen

REEDSWAIN BOOKS and VIDEOS
612 Pughtown Road
Spring City, Pennsylvania 19475 USA
1-800-331-5191 • www.reedswain.com

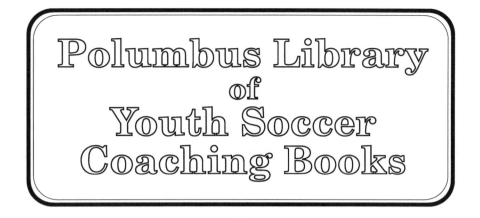

Practical coaching tools for developing quality youth and youth soccer programs

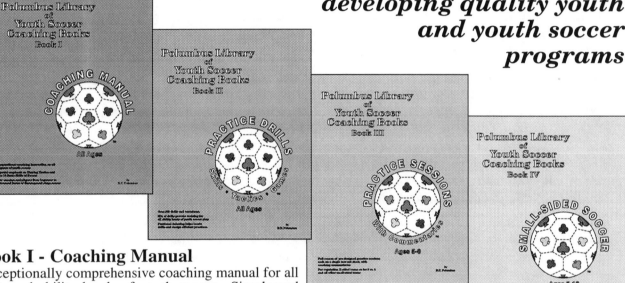

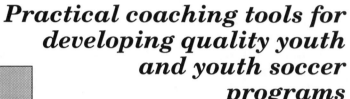

Book I - Coaching Manual

Exceptionally comprehensive coaching manual for all ages and ability levels of youth soccer. Simple and easy-to-understand with more than 80 quality photographs and illustrations. Designed primarily as a reference manual for finding detailed coaching instruction on the 10 Basic Skills of Soccer, positions, formations, plays and tactics, physical conditioning, development of a proper mental attitude and other matters. Excellent for parents and players as well as coaches.

Book II - Practice Drills

A collection of more than 275 practice drills and competitive games for building winning teams. Clear descriptions and quality illustrations. Drills offer progressive variations beginning with simple repetitions and adding degrees of difficulty in steps. For beginners through advanced players of all ages. Special indexing provides easy access to drills and a means of selecting drills for primary and secondary emphasis enabling the coach to design efficient practices using drills that develop multiple skills and disciplines.

Book III - Practice Sessions

A full season set of 20 carefully designed practice sessions. Each session contains a series of exercises, drills and games designed to provide a balance of fun, physical conditioning, development of soccer skills and playing tactics which flow smoothly together within the time you allot for practice. Each session is set forth on an easy-to-understand, single tear out page, to carry to practice in a pocket or on a clipboard. Comes with a Coaching Commentary for each session for the more dedicated coach. Will save the entry level coach 15 to 25 hours of practice preparation time over the course of the season and will send him to every practice well prepared.

Book IV - Small-Sided Soccer

Offers a simple but complete coaching plan for teams playing with less than 11 players on a side. Special emphasis on triangle and diamond formation playing tactics for 3 vs. 3 and 4 vs. 4 soccer. This book, when combined with Book III - Practice Sessions, offers the entry level coach an outstanding set of coaching tools for development stage players involved in small-sided soccer.

Thank you...

...for your interest in The Polumbus Library Of Youth Soccer Coaching Books. I love the game of soccer. I love coaching kids. And, frankly, I like it when my teams win.

You may be among the great number of interested and talented parents and singles considering coaching youth soccer. I am sure if you are to get involved in something, you want to do a respectable job. Your knowledge of the game of soccer is likely limited and the amount of time you have is probably limited as well. The purpose of these books is to help new coaches be immediately and continually effective without the need for significant research or the expenditure of a great deal of preparation time during the season. The more experienced coaches will benefit from the many detailed and specific instructions and practice drills directed at advanced players.

I am in my fourteenth year of coaching youth soccer. Because of the fast growing popularity of soccer and my belief in the value of athletics as a great life training experience for young people, I have compiled these books to help both coaches and players maximize the value of their soccer experience. A very small percentage of kids will ever use their youth soccer experience to go into collegiate or professional soccer. Yet this soccer experience can be of tremendous value in building character, confidence and a competitive spirit. As with any endeavor, the better job you can do the more rewarding the experience can be.

You'll find that each book in the "Library" has an independent purpose but works together with the other books to provide all the needs of the coach. The books have special features that allow a coach to advance his or her knowledge and coaching skills within time constraints that are reasonable for volunteer coaches. The goal is to help both the coach and the player to become the very best they can be.

In addition to the coaches and players, many parents really appreciate the combined emphasis on quality soccer along with strong player/coach and player/player relationships. I believe that the coach and the kids need to remember that they are play...ing soccer. Good sportsmanship, fun and encouragement need to share the "win the game" emphasis.

Clubs and administrators appreciate the impact the books have on recruiting new coaches and the opportunity the books offer clubs to standardize their coaching programs through the structured curriculum offered in the books. These books truly respond to the common concerns of perspective new coaches, "I know nothing about soccer or coaching.", "It takes to much time to coach."

I hope my effort in writing these books helps you experience the joys and satisfaction of coaching youth soccer. Please call or write if we can answer any questions or if we can be of assistance to you or your club.

Tad

Introduction

Practice Sessions

Following is a set of 20 Practice Sessions for use over a ten-week season conducting two practices per week. Each Practice Session is designed for removal from the manual and use at practice.

Prior to attending practice each day you should determine the length of your practice time. In the left hand margin of each Practice Session, fill in the exact time of day that you will begin practice and the exact time you will begin each drill or game within a practice session. Each drill or game of the practice has a recommended number of minutes set forth on the session form which is based upon a one hour practice schedule.

Each Practice Session has been designed to provide a proper balance of fun, physical conditioning, skill development, psychological development, tactic and strategy work as well as competition and game type playing experience. Over the course of the full season, the 20 Practice Sessions are also designed to implement a proper building-block approach to teaching soccer skills and the other components of a good coaching plan. See the Polumbus *Coaching Manual* (*Book I of the Polumbus Library of Youth Soccer Coaching Books*) for a more detailed discussion of the four major components of a good coaching plan and the building-block approach to coaching them.

This set of 20 Practice Sessions is appropriate for first, second and third year teams through the age of 8. It may be used for 3-sided teams or for any other short-sided teams and for 11-sided teams.

The set of 20 Practice Sessions is also appropriate for use as a form for preparing practice schedules for older children. Coaches with a few years experience can simply modify the enclosed practice sessions with drills and competitive games taken from the Polumbus *Practice Drills* (i.e. *Book II of the Polumbus Library of Youth Soccer Coaching Book*) that are more appropriate for the age and abilities of their players. By utilizing these forms and sticking with the order in which the skills are taught in the enclosed set, the coach can assure him or herself that all aspects of a good coaching plan will be covered, that they will be taught in a proper building block sequence and that every practice will be properly balanced between physical and mental conditioning, skill development, small group tactics and game condition experience.

Commentaries

This set of 20 Practice Sessions is sufficient within itself to conduct a full season of good practices without any further study or research by the coach. However, for those coaches who are interested, this book also contains a set of 20 Commentaries on the Practice Sessions (one Commentary for each of the 20 Practice Sessions) which is designed to provide supplemental coaching materials for the specific drills, skills and games covered by each Practice Session. By spending 10 to 20 minutes before each practice reviewing the appropriate Commentary, the coach can become significantly better prepared for coaching each day.

Flexibility of Practice Sessions

The Polumbus Practice Sessions are not intended as a pre-determined set of rigid instructions from which the coach should not vary. Obviously, the practice sessions do pre-plan the coach's entire season for him or her and they insure that the coach will be well prepared for every practice through the entire season. With these goals assured in advance, it is hoped that the coach will be able to relax and enjoy himself and use the knowledge he gains as he goes along through the season to modify and improve the Practice Sessions to fit his specific team and needs.

Use of "Multiple Practice Stations" to Shorten Lines

In coaching youth soccer, it is extremely important to keep your players active throughout the entire practice. It is a waste of very dear time to leave players standing in lines or on the sideline watching games unless you have a good reason for doing so.

The drills and games in this book encourage the use of "Multiple Practice Stations" whenever possible. Coaches are encouraged to limit the number of players at each Practice Station to the fewest players needed to run any drill or game. This minimizes the length of lines and maximizes the number of touches of the ball (or practice repetitions) for each player. Two Practice Stations instead of one more than doubles the effective practice time and touches for every player.

PRACTICE SESSIONS WITH COMMENTARIES

Summary Of Practice Sessions

Sessions 1-20

SESSION NUMBER	Main Theme	Secondary Emphasis	Small Group Activity	Large Group Activity
1.	Testing Drills	All Skills	None	Full Team Scrimmage
2.	Kicking	Dribbling	2 vs. 1 Scrimmage	Full Team Scrimmage
3.	Dribbling	Passing/Receiving (2-touch), Goal Kicks, Corner Kicks Ball Control & Shielding	1 vs. 1 Scrimmage	Full Team Scrimmage
4.	Shooting	Dribbling, Passing/Receiving (2-Touch), Triangle Tactics	2 vs. 2 Rapid Shooting, 4-Sided Shooting Game	3 vs 3. Scrimmage
5.	Passing	Dribbling	1-Touch Passing	Full Team Scrimmage
6.	Defense	Shooting, Goal Kicks	2 vs. 2 Scrimmage	Full Team Scrimmage
7.	Shielding	Passing/Receiving (2-touch), Juggling	1 on 1 Ball Possesion	Narrow Field Scrimmage
8.	Receiving/Shielding	Dribbling, Throw-Ins, Goal Kicks, Corner Kicks	1 vs. 1 Dribble Goal Game	Full Team Scrimmage
9.	Passing/Tactics	Dribbling, Triangle Tactics	2 vs. 1 Scrimmage	3 vs. 3 Scrimmage
10.	Shooting	Dribbling, Triangle Tactics	Center Goal Soccer	3 vs. 3 Scrimmage
11.	Passing	Dribbling, Goal-side Defensive Tactics	Corner Goals Scrimmage, Man-to-Man Scrimmage	3 vs. 3 Scrimmage
12.	Tackling	Dribbling, Passing, Throw-Ins, Corner Kicks	2 vs. 1 Scrimmage	Full Team Scrimmage
13.	General Skills	Shooting, Dribbling, Aggresiveness, Passing, Throw-Ins, Receiving, Triangle Tactics	3 vs. 3 Zone Scrimmage (Wing Attack Game)	3 vs. 3 Scrimmage
14.	Passing	Kicking Technique, Dribbling, Triangle Tactics	None	3 vs. 3 Scrimmage
15.	Ball Control	Passing,, Triangle Tactics, Goal Kicks, Corner Kicks, Throw-In Tactics	Ball Control In Groups Of 3	Full Team Scrimmage
16.	Set Play Tactics	Throw-Ins, Shooting, Dribbling, Passing	None	3 vs. 3 Scrimmage
17.	Combination	Dribbling, Shooting, Passing, Ball Control, Defensive Tactics, Decision-Making	2 vs. 1 Dribbling & Shooting Drill	Full Team Scrimmage
18.	Defense	Dribbling, Passing, Tackling Triangle Tactics	None	3 vs. 3 Scrimmage
19.	Passing	Receiving, Shooting, Wall Pass Tactics, Ball Control	3 vs. 3 Zone Scrimmage (Wing Attack Game)	Running Relays
20.	All Skills	Dribbling, Passing, Ball Shielding & Control,Shooting, Receiving, Decision-Making	1 vs. 1 Scrimmage	3 vs. 3 Scrimmage

Guide to Symbols and Graphics

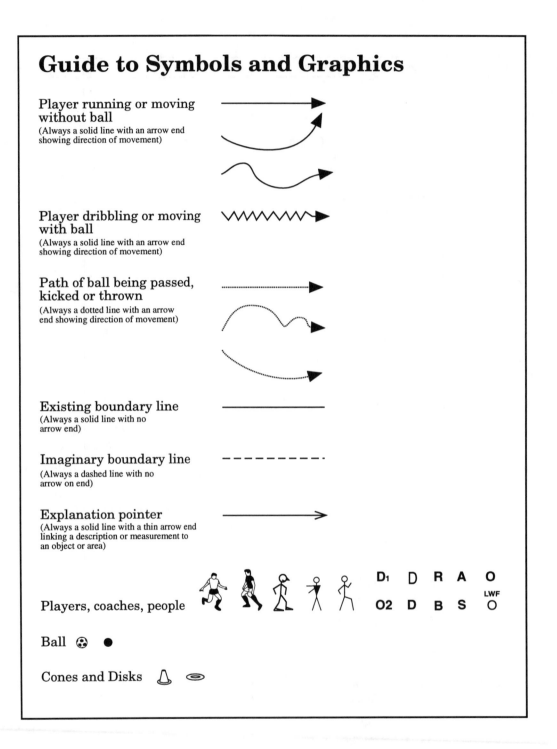

Player running or moving without ball
(Always a solid line with an arrow end showing direction of movement)

Player dribbling or moving with ball
(Always a solid line with an arrow end showing direction of movement)

Path of ball being passed, kicked or thrown
(Always a dotted line with an arrow end showing direction of movement)

Existing boundary line
(Always a solid line with no arrow end)

Imaginary boundary line
(Always a dashed line with no arrow on end)

Explanation pointer
(Always a solid line with a thin arrow end linking a description or measurement to an object or area)

Players, coaches, people   D₁ D R A O
                                O2 D B S O (LWF)

Ball

Cones and Disks

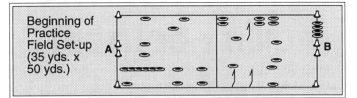

Beginning of Practice Field Set-up (35 yds. x 50 yds.)

Session 1

Start Times

I. Warm Ups

__:___ **A. General Discussion** (7 min.)

(1) Welcome. Purpose to have fun and learn how to play soccer.

(2) Rules of Practice. Must bring ball and shin guards and socks. Be good listeners if you want to be good players. Coach won't talk until everyone is quiet and listening.

(3) Rules of Game. Show kids marked field and goals etc. Purpose to kick ball into opponents goal and keep opponent from kicking ball into our goal. Kick with feet and legs and all parts of the body except the arms and hands. Do not worry yet about teaching specific local rules for your club.

II. Individual Skill Activities

(Theme: Testing Player's Abilities)

__:___ **A. Distance Kicking Contest** (10 min.)

3 to 5 kicks/player. Kick from goal line "A" (see diagram reverse side) lengthwise down field. Player stands by longest kick. Determine a "winner."

__:___ **B. Footrace Without Ball** (5 min.)

Determine fastest runners at 25 and 50 yds.

__:___ **C. Kick and Chase Ball** (8 min.)

Goal-line to goal-line (50 yds.), total of 7 times, 3 to 5 kids at a time. Both feet, right foot only, left foot only. End up with races.

__:___ **D. Water Break** (5 min.)

During water break set up agility course as shown on back side of this Practice Session One.

__:___ **E. Agility Contest** (15 min.) **(See Diagram Reverse Side)**

(1) Best to have approximately 4 coaches but can use a player for Coach No. 2 if necessary.

(2) Start approximately 1/3 of your players at Station 16 as shown on the diagram at the Accuracy Shooting Drill.

(3) Start the other players at Station 1 and have 2 players on the course at all times.

(4) Time all players for fun. Have all coaches note in writing the ability, speed and coordination of the players and compare the coaches notes after practice.

III. Small Group Activities

(None)

IV. Large Group Activities

__:___ **A. Full Team Scrimmage** (10 min.)

Divide into 2 teams of equal numbers of players. No coaching. No goalies. No throw-ins or goal kicks, etc. Coach keeps ball in play. Limit number of players per team to the number of players used in your regulation games. Run 2 scrimmages at same time if necessary to keep all players playing.

__:___ **End**

☞ *Before practice, mark off a field with lines or use cones to mark all corners and goals. Put most of the disc cones out that will be necessary for the agility contest but leave enough open space in middle to allow for drills II A, B, and C below.*

Equipment.
(1) 3 Plastic Cross Bars 5' to 6' long (corner flags will work)
(2) Two 12" cones and four 24" cones to support cross bars
(3) 30 pro-cones (discs)
(4) 4 cones 6 to 12" high
(5) Balls, 1 ball per player plus 4
(6) 2 stop watches

AGILITY CONTEST

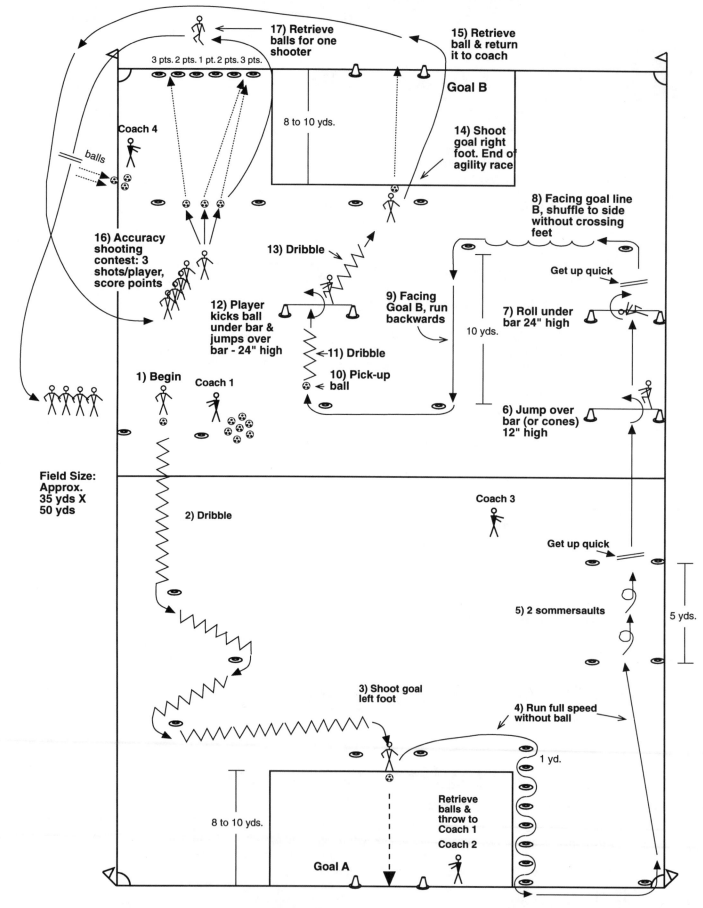

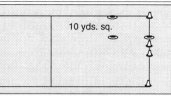

Beginning of Practice Field Set-up (35 yds. x 50 yds.)

10 yds. sq.

Start Times		Coaching Keys

I. Warm Ups

___:___ **A. <u>Kick and Chase</u>** (5 min.)

Goal-line to goal-line (50 yds.), total of 5 times, 3 to 5 kids at a time, both feet, right foot only, left foot only, use races to end drill.

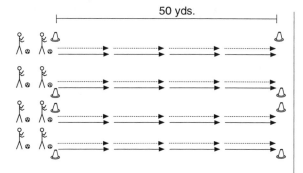

50 yds.

___:___ **B. <u>Over & Under Relay Race</u>** (5 min.)

Divide into 2 teams; each team line up single file; first player passes ball through legs to second player; second player passes ball over head to third player and so on to last player who runs to front of line and passes through legs, etc.; continue until everyone is back to where they started. Go 2 rounds if only few players.

___:___ **C. <u>Confined Area Dribbling</u>** (5 min.)

All players in small grid, e.g., 8 to 10 kids in 10 x 10 yd. grid. One ball per player. Dribble ball around in square without having a collision. Tell each kid he is a specific kind of expensive car (e.g., Porsche, Mercedes, etc.) and do not have a wreck; honking is permitted.

10 yd. sq. grid

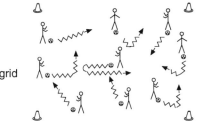

☞ *Keep ball close to feet, look where you are going; stay under control.*

___:___ **D. <u>Water Break</u>** (5 min.)

II. Individual Skill Activities

(Theme: Kicking)

___:___ **A. <u>Demonstration: Proper Kicking Technique</u>** (5 min.)

(1) Demo proper first step with non-kicking foot landing 6 to 9 inches beside center of ball. (Also demo improper kick with no step swinging kicking foot under body next to stationary non-kicking foot). (2) Demo 3 types of kicks, (a) inside foot, (b) outside foot, (c) instep or shoelaces.

☞ *Balance, proper steps, proper technique for each type of kick. Eyes on ball when kicking. See Commentary.*

___:___ **B. <u>Stationary Pairs Kicking</u>** (10 min.)

In pairs 8 to 10 yds. apart, practice kicking back and forth using inside foot and instep (shoelaces) types of kicks. Use proper kicking technique. See Commentary.

___:___ **C. <u>Water Break</u>** (5 min.)

During break set up 15 x 25 yd. grids for IIIA below.

III. Small Group Activity

Coaching
Keys

__:___ A. <u>2 vs. 1 Scrimmage</u> (10 min.)

Grid 15 x 25 yds. with goals but no goalies. Use proper kicking technique while passing and shooting during scrimmage. Run as many grids as are necessary to keep all players playing. Players alternate playing alone.

IV. Large Group Activity

__:___ A. <u>Full Team Scrimmage</u> (10 min.)

Divide players into 2 teams and have regular scrimmage. Watch kicking techniques but minimize coaching. Limit number of players per team to the number used in your regulation games. Run 2 scrimmages at same time if necessary to keep all players playing. Use your field size and rules if involved in a short-sided soccer league.

__:___ **End**

Beginning of Practice Field Set-up (35 yds. x 50 yds.)

10 yd. sq.

IB.

Session 3

I. Warm Ups

__:___ **A. Kick and Chase** (5 min.)

Goal-line to goal-line (50 yds.), total of 5 times, 3 to 5 kids at a time, both feet, right foot only, left foot only, use races to end drill.

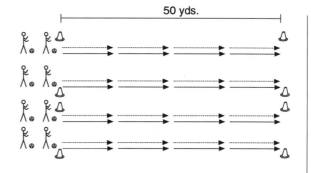

50 yds.

__:___ **B. Confined Area Dribbling** (5 min.)

All players in small grid e.g., 8 to 12 kids in 10 x 10 yd. grid. One ball per player. Dribble ball around in square without having a collision. Tell each kid he is a specific kind of expensive car (e.g., Porsche, Mercedes, etc.) and do not have a wreck, honking is permitted. Coach calls out "red light, green light, fast, slow, turn, etc."

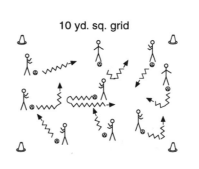

10 yd. sq. grid

☞ *Keep ball close to feet, eyes up (look where you are going), stay under control.*

__:___ **C. Scatter Game** (5 min.)

Using same square as in B above, players try to kick the other players balls out of the square and protect their own ball until only 1 player is left-- Who "wins"

__:___ **D. Two-Touch Passing** (8 min.)

(1) Demonstrate Two-Touch Passing (3 min.). First touch pushes ball just far enough in front and to the side of receiver to allow full pre-kicking step to be taken with non-kicking foot without need to move backwards or sideways to adjust for a return kick. Take pre-kicking step immediately after first touch to initiate the second touch. Second Touch is the pass.

__:___ *(2) Stationary Pairs Two-Touch Passing (5 min.), 8 yds. apart, kick back and forth practicing proper first touch, immediate step and return pass for second touch. Coach count out loud the two touches (i.e. "One"... pause ... "Two") in a smooth cadence encouraging an immediate step after the first touch.*

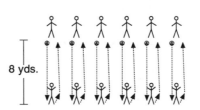

8 yds.

☞ *First touch is "most important touch in soccer." Always try for a "perfect first touch." See Commentary.*

__:___ **E. Water Break** (5 min.)

II. Individual Skill Activities

(Theme: Dribbling)

__:__   **A. <u>Destination /Speed Drill</u> (6 min.)**

Dribble to a cone and back as fast as you can 20-30 yds. Maximum 2 players to a line (see diagram).

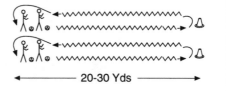

__:__   **B. <u>Control Dribbling Drill</u>   (6 min.)**

Weave through 15 cones placed 3 to 6 yds. apart, in a straight line, total of 3 to 5 times. Run 2 drills at same time - 1/2 of players in each drill.

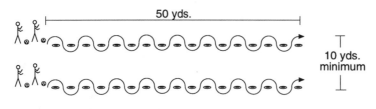

Cones are 3 yds. apart

__:__   **C. <u>Water Break</u> (5 min.)**

During water break set up grids for IIIA below.

III. Small Group Activity

__:__   **A. <u>1 vs. 1 Scrimmage</u> (5 min.)**

Grids 15 x 25 yds., no goalies, small goals. Minimize coaching but encourage dribbling and ball control. Run 3, one- minute periods with short rests in between. Run as many grids as are necessary to play all players at same time.

IV. Large Group Activity

__:__   **A. Full Team Scrimmage (10 min.)**

Divide into 2 equal teams. Regular scrimmage. Emphasize dribbling "control" in crowded areas (city driving) and dribbling "speed" in open areas (highway driving). Begin using goal kicks and corner kicks during scrimmage (but no positions or plays). Limit number of players per team to number used in your regulation games. Run two or more scrimmages at same time, if necessary, to keep all players playing. Use your own field size and rules if involved in small-sided soccer league.

__:__   **End**

Beginning of Practice Field Set-up (35 yds. x 50 yds.)

IB 10 yds.

IIA 15 yds.

IIIA&B

IIA 15 yds.

IVA

IVA

30 yds.

30 yds.

10 yds.

← 20 yds. →   10 yds.   ← 20 yds. →

Start Times

I. Warm Ups

Coaching Keys

__:__ **A. Wheel Barrow Nudge Race** (5 min.)

One player holds feet of partner who walks on hands and nudges ball with nose or head to a line. Change positions and go back to beginning. Teams of 2 race each other.

__:__ **B. Two-Touch Passing Drill** (7 min.)

Set up a series of practice stations; 4 players per station. At each station have two lines facing each other in single file, 10 yds. apart. Two players per line. First player in one line passes ball to first player in other line and runs to the back of the other line. Receiving player receives ball with first touch and passes ball back to next player in the other line for second touch and runs to the back of the other line, etc.

☞ *Make first touch perfect. Step immediately to ball for second touch.*

← 10 yds. →

Line A   Line B

__:__ **C. Throw-In- Practice** (8 min.)

Demonstrate: (1) 2 hands on ball; (2) ball held behind head; (3) throw ball straight overhead; (4) both feet on ground (even after the throw). Drill: half players on touchline (sideline) holding ball, throw in to partner (10 yds. away) who catches ball and does a throw-in back to original partner. Repeat.

☞ *Develop power with proper technique.*

10 Yds

II. Individual Skills Activities

(Theme: Shooting)

__:__ **A. Triple Shot Drill** (10 min.)

Three or four players per practice station. One or two shooters and two retrievers. Each player begins behind cone and runs to shoot ball No. 1 with right foot shoelaces. Player runs back around cone to shoot ball No. 2 with left foot shoelaces and then runs back around cone to shoot ball No. 3 with either foot and type of kick of player's choice.

☞ *Shoot hard and low with proper technique. Turn and run hard after each shot.*

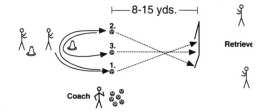

├─ 8-15 yds. ─┤

2.
3.
1.

Retriever

Coach

__:__ **B. Water Break** (5 min.)

III. Small Group Activity

__:___ **A. 2 vs. 2 Rapid Shooting Drill** (5 min.)

2 goals 10 yds. apart. Grid 10 yd. square. Two teams with 2 players each. Each team can only score in its own goal. Coach throws in new ball every time a shot is taken or ball leaves grid. Run as many grids as necessary to be sure all players are playing the full time.

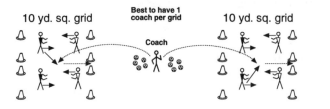

__:___ **B. Four Sided Shooting Game** (5 min.)

Using two of the same grids as in IIIA, set up 1 goal (5 ft. wide) on each side of the 4 sides of each grid. Divide players into 2 teams for each grid (minimum 6 players per grid) with colored jerseys. Score as many goals as possible in any goal. Coach serves up a new ball and shouts out score every time a goal is scored or the ball leaves the grid.

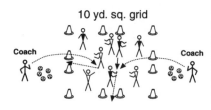

☞ *Keep balls coming fast. Stop play occasionally and praise the aggressive players.*

IV. Large Group Activity

__:___ **A. Water Break: Discussion of Triangles: 3 vs. 3 Scrimmage** (15 min.)

While players have water break, have a short (5-7 min.) discussion about triangles and position responsibilities in triangle formations (see Coaching Commentary for this Practice Session). Then, using as many 20x30 yard grids as are necessary to keep all players playing (6 players per grid), scrimmage 3 vs 3. Theme for scrimmage: provide front and rear support for player with ball and shoot, shoot, shoot.

☞ *Keep it simple. See Commentary.*

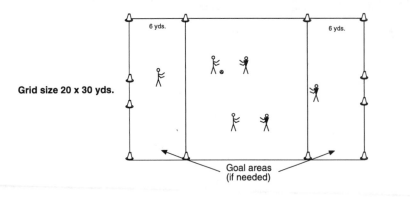

__:___ **End**

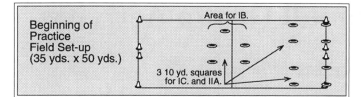

Beginning of
Practice
Field Set-up
(35 yds. x 50 yds.)

Area for IB.

3 10 yd. squares
for IC. and IIA.

Session
5

Tear out along perforation.

Start Times		Coaching Keys

I. Warm Ups

__:___ **A. Body Parts Game**   (5 min.)

All players lie spread eagled on stomach on ground. Coach calls out different body parts which are only parts that can touch ground. Have players walk like crabs or on all fours and have one player try to tag another player. Throw ball out.

☞ *Stretching, balance, agility.*

__:___ **B. Dribbling and Reaction Drill**   (5 min.)

Randomly spread out half as many cones as players. Players dribble randomly. On whistle players leave ball and run to a cone. Only 2 players to a cone.

☞ *Quick reaction movement and decision-making.*

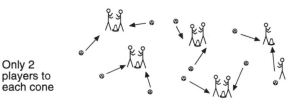

Only 2 players to each cone

__:___ **C. Keep Away**   (10 min.)

Set up as many practice stations (10x10 yd. square grids) as are necessary for 4 players per station. (1) (5 min.) 3 on 1 keep away using hand passing of the ball in the grids. Offensive player who loses ball becomes defender. (2) (5 min.) 3 on 1 keep away using feet passing (i.e. kicking) in same grid. Offensive player who loses ball becomes defender.

☞ *Body movement to get open. Kids will do it naturally in hand passing but not in feet passing.*

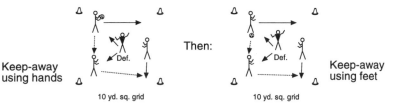

Keep-away using hands

Then:

Keep-away using feet

10 yd. sq. grid   10 yd. sq. grid

__:___ **D. Water Break**   (5 min.)

II. Individual Skill Activities

(Theme: Passing)

__:___ **A. Confined Area Passing**   (10 min.)

Place 5 pairs of players in each 10 yd. square. Each pair has 1 ball. Hand Passing with all players moving in the grid. After 5 minutes change to foot passing (i.e., kicking) with all players moving in the grid. Go back and forth from hands to feet.

10 yd. sq. grid

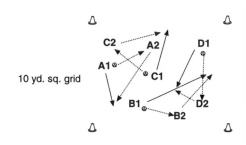

☞ *Eyes up. Avoid collisions with people or balls. Make good choices for passes.*

__:___ **B. Water Break**   (5 min.)

__:___ **A. <u>One Touch Passing Drill</u>** **(10 min.)**

Players in circle with coach (or a player) in middle (5 to 7 yd. radius): Coach passes balls to players who use a one touch return pass to coach. See how many in a row the kids can get back. Maximum 5 or 6 players on circle at each playing station.

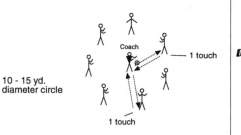

10 - 15 yd.
diameter circle

☞ *Control distance and accuracy with inside of foot pass.*

<u>IV. Large Group Activity</u>

☞ *Spread out. Get open. Move without the ball. Support your teammates with the ball.*

__:___ **A. <u>Full Team Scrimmage (Limit on Touches: Min. Passes)</u>** **(10 min.)**

Divide players into 2 teams and scrimmage. Field size 1/2 to 3/4 of regulation soccer field. Use 2 or 3 touch limits and/or experiment with minimum number of passes before a shot. Be sure to allow some time for regular scrimmage near end of period.

__:___ **End**

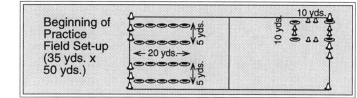

I. Warm Ups

Start Times — *Coaching Keys*

A. Ball Touch Drill (1 min.)

Straddling the ball, hop from 1 foot to the other touching the top of ball lightly with bottom of foot that is off the ground. Weight must be all on foot on the ground.

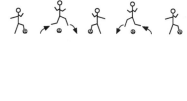

☞ *See how fast kids can go.*

B. Ball Hop (1 min.)

Hop over ball, side to side, holding both feet together.

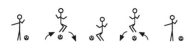

C. Four-Sided Shooting Game (5 min.)

Using a grid 10 yds. x 10 yds. for 8 to 10 players set up one small goal (5 feet wide) on each of 4 sides. Divide players into 2 teams. Score goals. Coach keep balls in play and calls out score every time a goal is made or ball leaves the grid.

10 yd. sq. grid

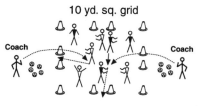

☞ *Reward the aggressive players with praise.*

II. Individual Skill Activities
(Theme: Defense)

A. Goal-side Position Drill Without Ball (10 min.)

With cones create a series of practice stations, each with a lane 5 yds. wide, 10-20 yds. long with a goal at one end. Maximum 6 players per station. No balls. Offensive player tries to run past defensive player to the goal without leaving the lane or illegally "charging" the defensive player. Defensive player tries to maintain "goal-side" position (i.e., on a line between offensive player and the center of the goal) forcing offensive player out the side of the lane and preventing him from reaching the goal. Rotate from offense to defense after each run.

☞ *Quick feet. Play defense by moving feet into goal-side position not by tackling the ball with your feet. Keep lanes narrow enough to guarantee success for the defenders.*

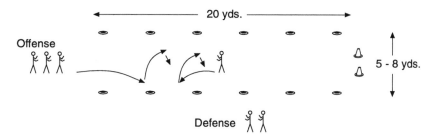

Tear out along perforation.

Copyright © 1992, 1994 by R. T. Polumbus

__:___ **B. <u>Goal-side Position Drill With Ball</u> (10 min.)**
Repeat drill A with ball and widen lane to 8-10 yds.

__:___ **C. <u>Water Break</u> (5 min.)**
During water break set up grids for IIIA below.

III. Small Group Activity

__:___ **A. <u>2 vs. 2 Scrimmage</u> (8 min.)**
Set up enough narrow grids (10 x 20 yds) for 4 players per grid for entire team. Scrimmage 2 vs. 2 emphasizing playing defense in goal-side position. For odd numbers of players have 1 field play 2 vs. 1 or 3 vs. 2.

IV. Large Group Activity

__:___ **A. <u>Full Team Scrimmage (Goal Kick Practice)</u> (20 min.)**
Divide players into 2 teams. Scrimmage with goalies on a field 1/2 to 3/4 of a regulation size soccer field. Kick all goal kick opportunities and spread non-kickers out evenly across the field, 18 yds. in front of the ball, to receive the goal kick. Goalie should not take the goal kicks.

__:___ **End**

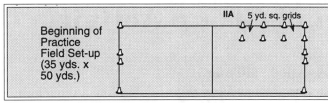

Beginning of
Practice
Field Set-up
(35 yds. x
50 yds.)

**Session
7**

Tear out along perforation.

I. Warm Ups

__:___ **A. Running and Reaction Drill (2 min.)**

Players line up side by side on goal line. No balls. Coach uses whistle. One whistle means run slowly. Two whistles run fast. Three whistles reverse direction and run fast.

☞ *Coach gives them long runs, short runs, explosions, 2 quick reverses, etc.*

__:___ **B. Two Touch Passing Drill (5 min.)**

Set up a series of practice stations; 4 players per station. At each station have two lines facing each other in single file, 10 yds. apart. Two players per line. First player in one line passes ball to first player in other line and runs to the back of the other line. Receiving player receives ball with first touch and passes ball back to next player in the other line for second touch and runs to the back of the other line, etc.

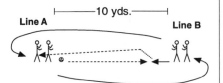

☞ *First touch is most important. Make it perfect placing ball 3 feet away and slightly to one side of receivers feet. Step immediately with non-kicking foot to initiate the second touch return pass.*

__:___ **C. Ball Touch and Juggling (3 min.)**

Straddling the ball, hop from 1 foot to the other touching the top of the ball lightly with the bottom of the foot that is off the ground. Every 15 seconds have each player hold ball between his feet and try to hop up and throw ball into air and promptly return to ball tap.

II. Individual Skill Activities

(Theme: Shielding)

__:___ **A. Ball Shielding (15 min.)**

Two equal lines of players at each practice station as shown. Each line stands outside a 5 yd. square grid on adjacent sides of the grid. Coach, or player/server, stands outside the square on opposite side from line 1. Coach serves a ball to first player in line 1 who receives it inside the square and tries to keep ball inside square shielding it from first player in line 2. Line 2 player must delay his run until receiver has touched the ball. Player should not play against same opponent every time.

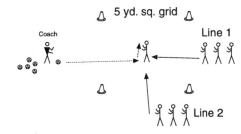

☞ *Keep body between ball and opponent not facing either one (e.g., Keep the player on your right side and ball on your left side or vice versa). Lots of quick touches of the ball and changes of body position.*

__:___ **B. Water Break (5 min.)**

During water break set up grids for III A and IV A.

III. Small Group Activity

__:___ **A. <u>One on One Ball Possession</u>** (**10 min.**)

Set up enough 5-7 yd. square grids for your entire team, 2 players in each grid. One player dribbles and shields the ball as long as possible in grid. Other player tries to take ball away. Reverse roles when ball is lost to other player. Play 1 minute then rest 30 seconds, repeat etc. for a total of 6 playing periods. After 3 playing periods exchange partners with other grids.

5 - 7 yd. sq. grid

IV. Large Group Activity

__:___ **A. <u>Narrow Field Scrimmage</u>** (**20 min.**)

Divide players into 2 equal teams. Using a field approx. 20 x 50 yds., have a regular scrimmage. Limited width should encourage opportunities for ball shielding and need for ball control.

__:___ **End**

Beginning of Practice Field Set-up (35 yds. x 50 yds.)	5 yds.	5 yds.	5 yds.	5 yds.
	5 yds.	5 yds.	5 yds.	5 yds.

Session 8

Tear out along perforation.

Start Times	# I. Warm Ups	**Coaching Keys**

__:___   **A. Brazilian Jog** (5 min.)

Two single file lines standing side-by-side. Players "jog" wherever the first 2 players lead them for 5 minutes. As they jog, "coach" (or front 2 players) calls out "right hand" and all players touch ground with right hand. Left hand, both hands, header jumps, skip, front roll, etc. and players respond.

☞ *After players understand drill, let them call out directions.*

__:___   **B. Receive and React** (5 min.)

Working in pairs with player 1 standing 2 yds. on one side of a cone goal 5 yards wide and player 2 standing 5 to 10 yds. in front of goal on opposite side. Player 1 shuffles back and forth to outside of each cone. Player 2 serves ball to player 1 each time player 1 reaches the outside of a cone. Player 1 uses 2 touch reception and return pass to player 2. Serve grounders, bouncers, and air balls. Alternate roles every 10 receptions.

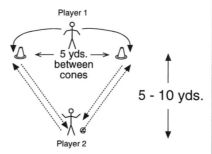

☞ *Serves should be easy for receiver to handle. Coaches may need to act as servers and let player 2 wait n line behind goal.*

__:___   **C. Serve and Defend** (5 min.)

Use same pairs and stations as in B above. Player 1 stands in goal and serves ball to player 2 who is 10 yards in front of goal. Player 1 follows serve and defends the goal. Player 2 must "receive the pass" and try to score a goal. Play until goal is scored or ball is turned over to defender. Rotate positions every 10 serves. Vary the serves to encourage chest and thigh receptions as well as foot receptions.

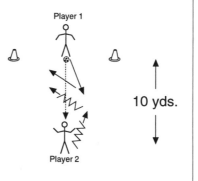

☞ *Servers must make good serves that give receiver plenty of time to make a clean reception and gain control of ball before server arrives to defend.*

__:___   **D. Water Break** (5 min.)

During water break set up grids for IIB and IIIA below.

II. Individual Skill Activities
(Theme: Receiving/Shielding)

__:___   **A. Ball Shielding Demonstration** (5 min.)

Coach demonstrates receiving a ball using first touch to move ball away from defender and moving his body between the ball and the defender to shield the ball. Be sure players understand importance of coach's body facing sideways, with ball on his right or left side and the defender on his other side (i.e., ball should not be in front or behind the player shielding the ball). Also demonstrate legs spread wide and legal shoulder-to-shoulder body contact for pushing and leverage.

☞ *Use the grid and player alignments for drill IIB below to demonstrate proper technique.*

B. <u>Ball Shielding Drill</u> (10 min.)

Two lines of players at each station (6 players per station). Each line stands outside a 5 yd. square grid on adjacent sides of the grid. Coach or player/server stands outside the square on opposite side from line 1. Coach serves a ball to first player in line 1 who receives it inside the square and tries to shield ball from first player in line 2. Line 2 player must delay his run until receiver has touched the ball. Players should not play against the same opponent all the time.

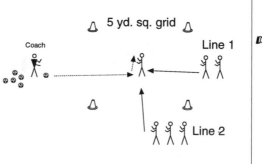

☞ *First touch by receiver must move ball toward side of grid opposite line 2 and receiver must use proper shielding technique described in IIA above.*

III. Small Group Activity

A. <u>1 vs. 1 Dribble Goal Game</u> (5 min.)

Four pairs of players per 15 yard square grid. One goal (2 yds. wide) on each side of grid. Each pair has a ball and plays 1 vs. 1. Player with ball tries to score by "dribbling" through any goal (i.e., not shooting) from inside the square to outside. Other player defends, tries to tackle ball and score a "dribbling goal" himself. Players need not stay inside square. Keep score. Give players a 30-second break every minute or so to encourage their full effort while playing.

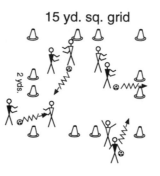

☞ *Ball control and shielding should be used to gain advantages. Encourage feints and fakes.*

B. <u>Water Break</u> (5 min.)
During water break set up field for IVA below.

IV. Large Group Activity

A. <u>Full Team Scrimmage</u> (15 min.)

Divide players into 2 equal teams and scrimmage. Use throw-ins, goal kicks and corner kicks when appropriate but do not interrupt play to coach set play positions or tactics. Limit number of players per team to the number used in your regulation games. Run 2 scrimmages if necessary to keep all players playing. Use your own field size and rules if involved in small-sided soccer.

End

Session 9

Beginning of Practice Field Set-up

3 yds.   3 yds.
6 yds.
Grid 15 yds. x 25 yds.   10 yds. apart   Grid 15 yds. x 25 yds.
6 yds.   5 yds.   5 yds.

Start Times

I. Warm Ups

Coaching Keys

__:___ **A. Ball Touch Drill** **(1 min.)**

All players stand with ball on ground between feet. Hop from 1 foot to the other touching the top of the ball lightly with the bottom of the foot that is off the ground. Every 10 touches throw ball in air, retrieve and repeat.

__:___ **B. Ball Hop** **(1 min.).**

Hop over ball with both feet side-to-side, then forward and backwards.

__:___ **C. Jog Around Outside of Full Field** **(3 min.)**

2 single file lines, players side by side.

__:___ **D. Circle Passing** **(15 min.)**

Form several circles 10-15 yds. in diameter with 6 to 7 players per circle. (a) 3 min.--pass ball across circle, call out name of intended receiver; (b) 3 min.--same as (a) except follow your pass and take receiver's spot in circle (c) 3 min.--same as (b) except use 2 balls; (d) 6 min.--same as (a) except use 1 or 2 defenders in center of circle. Defenders change positions with last player to touch ball on an interception.

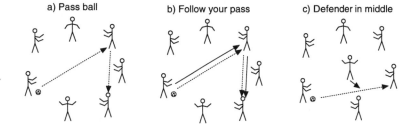

10 - 15 yd. diameter circles

a) Pass ball   b) Follow your pass   c) Defender in middle

II. Individual Skill Activities

(Theme: Passing)

__:___ **A. Full Team Keep-Away** **(5 min.)**

Using a large grid (1/2 of regulation field for 14 to 18 players) divide players into 2 teams. Use colored bibs. Play keep away. Coach keeps score. 1 point for 3 (4 or 5) consecutive passes by either team. Min. 10 yds. distance between players. Avoid bunching.

☞ *Coach counts passes out loud. Keep it exciting.*

__:___ **B. Water Break** **(5 min.)**

During water break set up grids for IIC below.

Tear out along perforation.

___:___   **C.** <u>**2 vs. 1 Scrimmages**</u>   **(15 min.)**

Divide players into groups of 3. Set up as many 15 x 25 yd. grids as are necessary to place 2 groups (6 players) on each grid. One group scrimmages 2 vs. 1 while the other group acts as ball retrievers and quickly throws a new ball in every time ball leaves the goal. Every 2 minutes change groups. Players alternate playing alone. Be sure the single player always goes toward the large goal. Require 2 or 3 touch passing by team with 2 players.

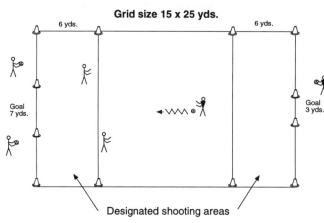

Grid size 15 x 25 yds.

Designated shooting areas

☞ *Allow shooting only from within the designated shooting areas.*

___:___   **D.** <u>**Water Break**</u>   **(5 min)**

During water break, set up field for IVA below.

III. Small Group Activity
(None)

IV. Large Group Activities

___:___   **A.** <u>**3 vs. 3 scrimmage**</u>   **(10 min.)**

Divide players into 3 man teams. Use as many 20 x 30 yd. grids as are necessary to accommodate all players at the same time. Scrimmage 3 vs. 3 emphasizing positions (fielder with ball and front and rear support fielders) and responsibilities and minimum 10 yds. between players. After 5 min. limit to 1 or 2 touch passing or require minimum 3 passes before a shot, or require one back pass with a switch of ball to opposite side of field, etc. Use your own field size and rules if involved in a 3-sided soccer league.

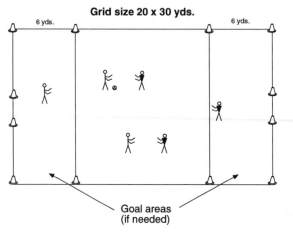

Grid size 20 x 30 yds.

Goal areas
(if needed)

___:___   **End**

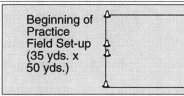

Beginning of Practice Field Set-up (35 yds. x 50 yds.)

20-25 yds.

I. Warm Ups

__:___   **A.** <u>**Kick and Chase Races with Stop Whistle**</u>   (5 min.)

In groups of 4 to 6 players conduct 50 yd. dribbling races (i.e., kick and chase). Advise players that on coach's whistle, they must immediately stop running and trap the ball on the ground with the sole of one foot. On coach's second whistle, players continue the race.

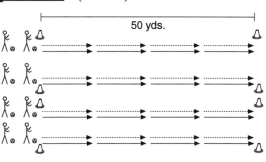

50 yds.

☞ *Do not blow whistle in every race. Players must keep ball close enough to stop within 3 steps after whistle.*

__:___   **B.** <u>**Jog Around Outside of Full Field**</u>   (3 min.)

Two single file lines, players side-by-side.

__:___   **C.** <u>**Round the Cones and Shoot**</u>   (10 min.)

Set up cones in front of goal as shown in diagram. Players form 2 lines in middle of field. One at a time players run around the cones and back toward ball which has been "centered" by the coach (or player/server) on opposite side of goal, for a shot by player. One touch shots. Instep (or shoe laces) shots only. Players rotate from shooting line to retriever to the other shooting line. Coach changes point of serve to corner of field after 5 minutes.

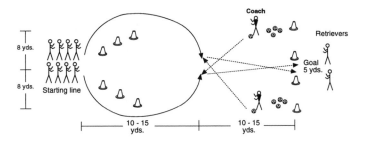

__:___   **D.** Water Break   (5 min.)

During water break, set up cones for IIA and IIIA below.

II. Individual Skill Activities

(Theme: Shooting)

__:___   **A.** <u>**Continuous Shooting Drill**</u>   (7 min.)

Using 2 lines of shooters (A & B), 2 retrievers and 2 servers (coaches) as shown on diagram, players begin in line A, run around cone A and back toward goal.

Server 1 serves ball as shown for a 1-touch shot by player. Player rotates to retriever for 2 shots then to Line B where he runs around cone B for a shot served by Server 2. After shot from line B player returns to Line A and continues cycle.

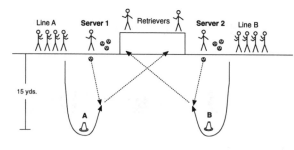

☞ **Use hard shots to corners of goal, empha-size shoelace kicks.**

__:___ **B. Shooting vs. Defender** (5 min.)

Use same arrangement of lines as in drill IIA above. However, line A has shooters and line B has defenders. Server 2 serves ball to shooter, who comes around cone A (see diagram). Player B starts a defensive run at moment the server kicks the ball and at-tempts to block the shot by player A. Players rotate from line A, to retriever for 2 shots, to line B and back to line A. Run drill from both sides.

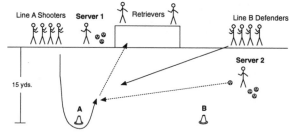

☞ **Defenders must wait until server kicks ball to leave. Shooters must make accu-rate, but hard 1-touch shots quickly to avoid defend-er.**

III. Small Group Activity

__:___ **A. Center Goal Soccer** (10 min.)

Set up as many 20 x 30 yd. grids as are necessary to play all your players at the same time with 7 players per grid (3 vs. 3, plus 1 goalie). Place one goal 6 yds. wide, in the center of each field as shown with a goalie in the goal. The team going east must score from west to east through the goal and vice versa for the team going west. Goalie is neutral. After a save the goalie distributes ball to opposite side of goal from where the shot came.

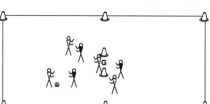

__:___ **B. Water Break** (5 min.)

During water break, set up cones for IVA below

IV. Large Group Activity

__:___ **A. 3 vs. 3 Scrimmage** (10 min.)

Using the same grids as in IIIA above, except remove center goal and add 3 yard goals at each end of each field, scrimmage 3 vs. 3 em-phasizing positions (fielder with ball and front and rear support fielders) and responsibilities and minimum 10 yds. between players. Encour-age long shots and lots of shooting. Use your own field size and rules if involved in a 3-sided soccer league.

Grid size 20 x 30 yds.

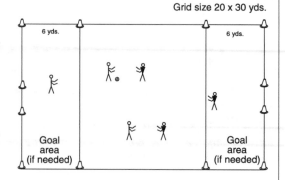

__:___ **End**

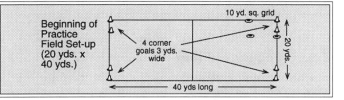

Start Times		Coaching Keys

I. Warm Ups

__:___ **A. Confined Area Dribbling** (10 min.)

Place players in a confined area marked out by cones. Everyone with a ball. Dribble ball inside the area without having a collision. Fast, slow, medium, reverse, left, right, etc. Coach calls out numbers and players respond. #1--Switch balls with someone. #2--Throw ball in air and retrieve. #3--Ball touch drill for 10 touches. #4--Scatter game (i.e., protect ball and kick other balls out of square).

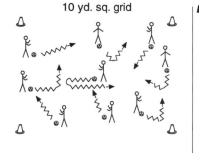

10 yd. sq. grid

☞ *Many quick changes of direction, reverses and speed variations. Keep ball close, eyes up, glance over shoulder to see where everyone is.*

__:___ **B. Scrimmage With Corner Goals** (6 min.)

Divide players into 2 equal teams. Set up grid as shown in diagram with 4 goals as shown. Team A may score in either of goals A1 or A2 and Team B may score in either of goals B1 or B2. Coach quickly throws in a new ball every time ball leaves grid or goal is scored and calls out score. After 5 min. rest 1 or 2 min. then go to IC below.

Grid size 20 x 40 yds.
Goals 3 yds. wide

☞ *Coach must keep game moving fast with new balls.*

__:___ **C. Scrimmage-Man-to-Man** (5 min.)

Use same grid as in IB above, except use only 1 goal, centered at each end. Give each player on each team a "man" on the opposing team to defend. The only person who can defend a player with the ball is that player's "man." All other rules are normal for scrimmage (i.e., use throw-ins, goal and corner kicks, etc.) except goals are scored by dibbling through the goal vs. shooting.

☞ *Emphasize staying with your man. Quickly get "goal-side" of "man" on turnover of ball to other team. Run, don't give up, work hard.*

__:___ **D. Water Break** (5 min.)

During break set up cone lanes for drill IID below.

II. Individual Skill Activities

(Theme: Passing)

__:___ **A. Two-Touch Passing Drill** (4 min.)

Set up an even number of practice stations with 3-5 players per station. The fewer players at each station the better. At each station have two lines facing each other in single file, 10 yds. apart. First player in one line passes ball to first player in other line and runs to the back of the other line. Receiving player receives ball with first touch and passes ball back to next player in the other line for second touch and runs to the back of the other line, etc.

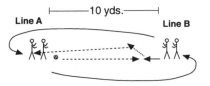

☞ *Emphasize good passes (accuracy and touch) and a "perfect first touch" on reception.*

___:___ **B.** <u>**Criss-Cross Two-Touch Passing**</u> **(5 min.)**

*Combine your playing stations in IIA above
into 1/2 as many stations with 2 groups of
players for each new station. Each group at
each station runs the Two-Touch Passing
Drill at right angles to the other group, criss-
crossing in the middle.*

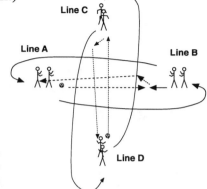

☞ *Concentrate
on job. Eyes
up, avoid colli-
sions with
balls or peo-
ple. Good
passes.*

___:___ **C.** <u>**Pairs Passing on the Run**</u> **(5 min.)**

*Divide players into pairs. Each pair passes
ball back and forth as they run 50 yds., staying
10 yds. apart. Players must strive to "keep
ball between them," being sure to use "outside
foot" to block path of ball on reception.*

☞ *"Lead" the re-
ceiver. Good
accuracy and
touch. Make
good first
touch on re-
ception.*

___:___ **D.** <u>**Two-Man Weave Inside Lane**</u> **(5 min.)**

*Stay in same pairs as IIC above. Using 5 yd. wide lanes marked out with cones, run
a 2-man pass and weave as shown in diagram.*

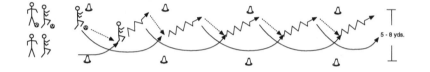

☞ *Tight con-
trolled drib-
bling and
passing. Soft
passes and
know how to
run weave.*

___:___ **E.** <u>**Water Break**</u> **(5 min.)**

During water break, set up field for IVA below.

III. Small Group Activity

(None)

IV. Large Group Activity

___:___ **A.** <u>**3 vs. 3 Scrimmage**</u> **(10 min.)**

*Divide players into 3-man teams. Use as many 20 x 30 yd. grids as are necessary to
accommodate all players at same time. Scrimmage 3 vs. 3 emphasizing positions;
rear and front support, minimum 10 yds. between players. Require 1 backwards
pass per attack. Use your own field size and rules if involved in a 3-sided soccer
league.*

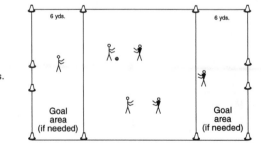

___:___ **End**

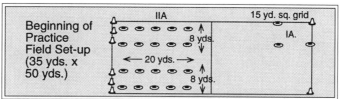

Start Times		Coaching Keys

I. Warm Ups

__:___ **A. Numbers Game** (10 min.)

Divide players into 2 teams (equal numbers) and line them up opposite each other as shown in diagram. Give each player on each team a number from 1 to the number of players on each team. Ball in middle of grid. Coach calls out 1 or more numbers and the players on both teams with those numbers run into grid attempting to gain control of the ball and to score a goal by shooting through opponent's side. Other players act as goalies (without hands) and try to keep ball on the grid.

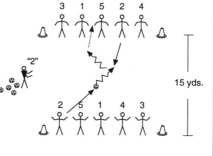

☞ *Any time ball leaves grid or a goal is scored, coach puts out a new ball and calls new numbers.*

__:___ **B. One-Step Tackle Practice** (3 min.)

In pairs each player stands one step away from ball facing opponent. On command of coach, each player steps forward planting non-kicking foot next to ball and tries to kick ball hard with instep, or inside of kicking foot, past his opponent. Repeat alternating feet.

__:___ **C. Jog Around Outside of Field** (3 min.)

Jog in 2 single file lines with pairs of players running shoulder to shoulder.

__:___ **D. Water Break** (5 min.)

During water break, set up grid for drills IIA below.

II. Individual Skill Activity

(Theme: Tackling)

__:___ **A. 1 on 1 Tackling Inside a Lane** (5 min.)

Form several practice stations as shown in diagram (4-7 players per station) with a line of offensive players and a line of defensive players as shown. As coach (or player/server) kicks ball to offensive player 01, D1 runs to defend against O1. O1 tries to dribble past D1 and on past the shooting line for a shot but must stay inside lane of cones. D1 attempts to tackle the ball to prevent shot.

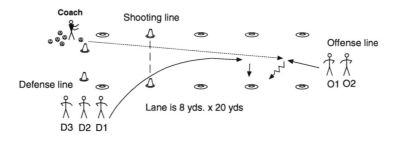

☞ *Engage, close and tackle in 3 separate stages. See Commentary.*

__:___ **B.** <u>First Variation on IIA</u> (5 min.)

Same grid. Move defensive line to where shown on diagram and let offensive player begin with the ball. On coach's whistle, O1 tries to dribble past shooting line and shoot and D1 gives ground trying to gain goal-side position, facing O1, and tackle ball.

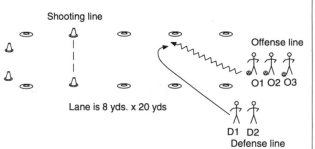

☞ *Be tough and aggressive on defense. Use legal physical contact, shoulder-to-shoulder.*

__:___ **C.** <u>Second Variation-Run Down From Behind</u> (5 min.)

Same grid. Place line of defenders 3 yds. behind line of offensive players as shown in diagram. On coach's whistle, O1 dribbles toward the shooting line for a shot.

D1 must run past O1, turn in front of him getting his shoulders goal-side of O1 and kick ball out the side of the lane. Defenders must aggressively turn into path of dribbler and not just run along side him.

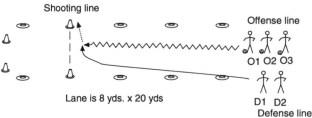

__:___ **D.** <u>Short Water Break</u> (4 min.)

During water break, set up grids for IIIA.

III. Small Group Activity

__:___ **A.** <u>2 vs. 1 Scrimmages</u> (8 min.)

Divide players into groups of 3. Set up as many 15 x 25 yd. grids as are necessary to place 2 groups (6 players) on each grid. One group scrimmages 2 vs. 1 while the other group acts as ball retrievers and quickly throws a new ball in every time ball leaves the field. Shooting allowed only within "shooting areas." Every 2 minutes change groups. Players alternate playing alone. Be sure single player always goes toward large goal. Require 2 or 3 touch passing by team with 2 players.

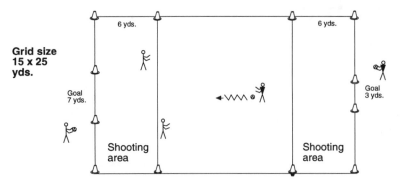

☞ *Emphasize good tackling by the 2-man team and good goalside position by the 1-man team.*

__:___ **B.** <u>Short Water Break</u> (2 min.)

During water break, set up grid for IVA .

IV. Large Group Activity

__:___ **A.** <u>Full Team Scrimmage</u> (10 min.)

Divide players into 2 equal teams and play regulation scrimmage. Use throw-ins, goal and corner kicks. Do not stop play but encourage proper positions on set plays.

__:___ **End**

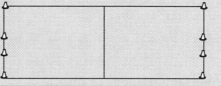

Session 13

<table>
</table>

Start Times

I. Warm Ups

Coaching Keys

Tear out along perforation.

__:__ A. <u>Jog Around Outside of Field</u> (3 min.)

Jog in 2 single file lines with pairs of players shoulder-to-shoulder.

__:__ B. <u>In-Your-Face Drill--1 vs. 1 vs. 1 Shooting</u> (15 min.)

Set up a practice station at each of 2 goals with 6-9 players per station. At each station form 3 lines of players 25 yds. in front of goal as shown in diagram. Goalie optional. Coach starts drill by kicking ball into area in front of players. First player in each line sprints for ball and tries to control it and shoot a goal. Each player without the ball tries to prevent shot and gain control of ball for himself and shoot a goal. Every time a goal is scored, or ball leaves the grid, coach quickly kicks in a new ball. Each set of 3 players keep playing for 7 balls. Players then rotate to retrievers and from retrievers to end of lines.

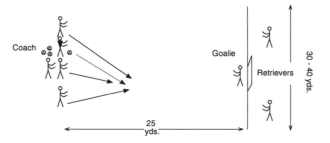

__:__ C. <u>Water Break</u> (5 min.)

During break, set up practice stations for IIA, B and C.

II. Individual Skill Activities
(Theme: General Skills)

__:__ A. <u>Multi-Skill Drill--One-Touch Shot</u> (5 min.)

Set up several practice stations with 7-9 players per station. At each station form 2 lines of players as shown in diagram, each player with a ball. Coach acts as server. A1 begins drill by executing a throw-in to the coach and running around cone to outside. Coach receives throw-in with foot, thigh or chest reception and lays pass out to side for A1 to execute a 1 touch instep (shoelaces) shot with his right foot. A1 rotates to retriever for 1 shot and then to end of line B. B1 then proceeds in same manner as A1 except to left side for left footed shot and then goes to retriever then to end of line A.

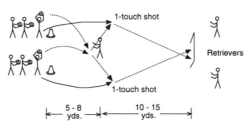

B. <u>Multi-Skill Drill--Two-Touch Shot</u> (5 min.)

Exact same drill as IIA above except players use first touch on pass from coach to "control" ball and set up a 2-touch shot.

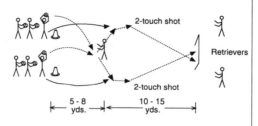

C. <u>Multi-Skill Drill--Players Act as Servers</u> (7 min.)

Exact same drill as IIB except players act as server to practice receptions. Alternate server every 5-10 shots. Use 2 touch shots unless coach calls for 1 touch. Servers must concentrate on making good receptions and coach should cause throwers to throw air balls for chest receptions, ground balls for foot receptions, etc.

D. <u>Water Break</u> (5 min.)

During water break set up grids for IIIA below.

III. Small Group Activity

A. <u>Zone Scrimmage--3 vs. 3</u> (10 min.)

Mark out as many 20 x 30 yd. grids as are necessary to accommodate all players at same time, 6 players to a grid. Use 3 yd. goals at each end of grids. Mark wing are-as with row of cones as shown in diagram. Players A1 and B1 must stay in middle zone and players A2 and B2, and A3 and B3 must stay in their respective wing zones. Scrimmage 3 vs. 3. If necessary to get more passes limit to 3 or 4 touches or require 1 or 2 passes to wing areas before shot.

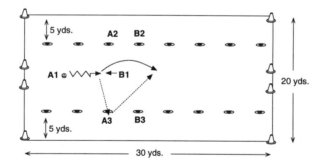

IV. Large Group Activity

A. <u>3 vs. 3 Scrimmage</u> (5 min.)

Remove the zone "cones" from all grids in IIIA above and continue 3 vs. 3 scrimmages. Give players "positions" and emphasize rear and front support responsibilities, minimum 10 yds. between players and patient confident control of ball. Use throw-ins, goal and corner kicks. Use your own field size and rules if involved in a 3-sided soccer league.

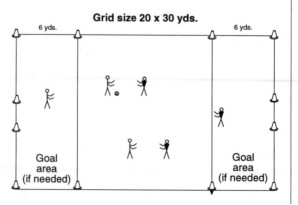

End

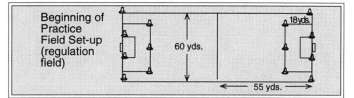

I. Warm Ups

__:__ **A. Change Direction Running** (3 min.)

Spread players out (3 to 4 yds. between players) in 2 to 4 lines (5 yards between lines). No balls. Coach stands at mid-field and points direction players are to run (e.g. forward, backward, right, left, diagonally, etc.). Players run as fast as they can making instant changes of direction at coach's signal.

__:__ **B. Reverse Direction Dribbling** (8 min.)

Line up 1/2 of players at each of 2 practice stations as shown in Diagram IB, every player with a ball. Players dribble to each cone in succession and do not go around cone, but turn their back to cone as they step over ball with proper foot to stop it and push it back in the reverse direction. Ball must completely cross penalty line and goal line. "Explode" with speed after direction change. Go backwards through course after all have gone one direction.

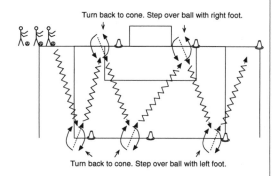

Turn back to cone. Step over ball with right foot.

Turn back to cone. Step over ball with left foot.

__:__ **C. Kicking Technique Practice: Stationary Ball** (7 min.)

Using same stations as IB, set up two single file lines of players with 2 retrievers as shown in diagram. Coach (or player) sets balls out for both lines for stationary kicks. 3 kicks per player using proper technique (i.e., eyes on ball at impact, proper step, follow through). Practice with both feet. Instep kicks, inside and outside of foot kicks, etc. Rotate from kicker to retriever to opposite line.

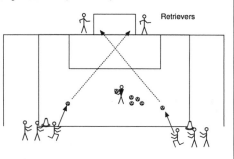

Retrievers

__:__ **D. Kicking Technique Practice: Moving Ball** (7 min.)

Same drill as IB except 2 servers pass ball from goal-line as shown in diagram. This is not a shooting drill. Players must concentrate on using proper "kicking technique."

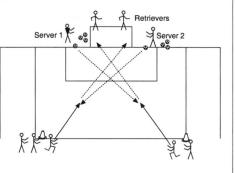

Server 1

Retrievers

Server 2

__:__ **E. Water Break** (5 min.)

II. Individual Skill Activities

(Theme: Passing)

__:__ **A. Find Target Before Ball Arrives** (5 min.)

Set up playing stations (30 x 30 yds.), 6-9 players per station as shown in diagram.

At each station set up 1 line of passers at mid-field line and one line of receivers beside the coach. Coach rolls ball to first player in the passing line who runs forward to pass the ball to the receiver. As ball is rolling to passer the receiver runs to his left or right and the passer must find him and make a good "1 touch" pass to him. "Eyes on ball" during kick. Rotate from Passer line to Receiver line to Passer line.

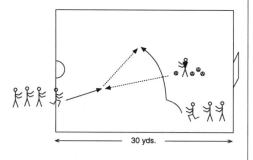

30 yds.

__:___ ### First Variation (5 min.)

Add a second receiver as shown. As coach rolls ball out, he calls out name of one of the two receivers and the passer must find that receiver and pass to her using "1-touch" pass..

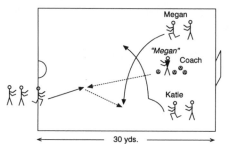

Megan

"Megan"   Coach

Katie

30 yds.

__:___ ### Second Variation (5 min.)

Use two receivers and one defender. Defender must "clearly" cover one of the two receivers and the passer must find the "open man."

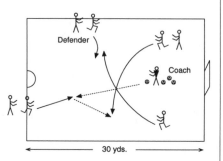

Defender

Coach

30 yds.

__:___ **B.** **Water Break** (5 min.)

During water break set up grids for IVA below.

III. Small Group Activity

(None)

IV. Large Group Activity

__:___ **A.** **3 vs. 3 Scrimmage** (10 min.)

Divide players into 3-man teams. Use as many 30 x 40 yd. grids as are necessary to accommodate all players at same time (i.e., 6 players per grid). Scrimmage 3 vs. 3 emphasizing positions, rear and front support for passing, minimum 10 yds. between players. Use your own field size and rules if involved in a 3-sided soccer league.

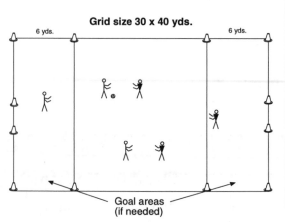

Grid size 30 x 40 yds.

6 yds.   6 yds.

Goal areas
(if needed)

__:___ **End**

Beginning of
Practice
Field Set-up

30 yds.

←20 yds.→   ←20 yds.→

Tear out along perforation.

I. Warm Ups

__:___ **A. Team Keep Away** (5 min.)

Divide players into 2 equal teams with colored bibs. On a large grid from 1/3 to 1/2 of a regulation field play keep away with each team trying to score points by making 3 (or 4, 5, etc.) consecutive passes without opponents touching ball. Coach counts passes out loud and calls out score.

__:___ **B. 3 vs. 3 Scrimmage** (10 min.)

Divide players into 3-man teams. Use as many 20 x 30 yd. grids as are necessary to accommodate all players at the same time. Scrimmage 3 vs. 3. Review responsibilities of each position (i.e. "rear support fielder," protect goal and provide rear support; "fielder with ball" penetrates by dribbling or passing or passes back; "front support fielder" provides forward support). Min. 10 yds. between players. Good tactics on throw-ins and goal and corner kicks.

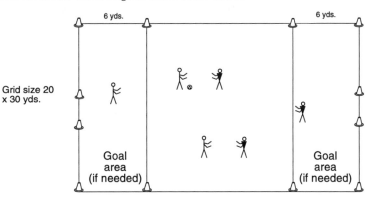

__:___ **C. Water Break** (5 min.)

II. Individual Skill Activities

(Theme: Ball Control)

__:___ **A. Ball Turnarounds** (5 min.)

At each of several practice stations as shown in diagram (4-6 players per station) set up a single file line of players. Coach rolls ball toward goal. Player must run down ball before it stops and turn it around and dribble through one of cone goals as shown. Do drill from both sides.

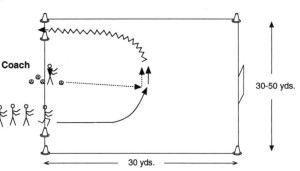

☞ *Player should not run around ball before reversing its direction. He should kick ball to sideline while running in direction of his own goal. Then retrieve ball and reverse direction.*

B. <u>**Ball Turnarounds with Opponent**</u> (5 min.)

Same set up as IIA except two lines of players. Line A tries to control ball and shoot goal at the far end of grid and line B tries to re- verse direction of ball and dribble through one of the cone goals near the starting line.

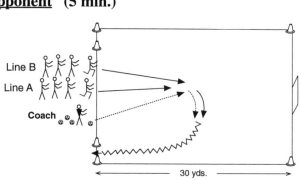

Line B

Line A

Coach

← 30 yds. →

III. Small Group Activity

A. <u>**Ball Control in Groups of 3**</u>

Divide players into groups of 3, one ball per group. Spread groups out across field. Each group of 3 lines up in a straight line with 1 player in the middle and 5 to 8 yds. between players.

(5 Min.) *Players on outside (A and C) alternate passing ball to middle player (B) who "receives" pass, turns ball around and passes it to the player behind him. Re- peat for 10 passes and rotate positions.*

☞ *Receiver al- ways "turns" to the side the ball arrives on.*

(8 Min.) *Player A passes ball to player B. Player C has option of running forward to defend (in which case A calls out "man-on" and B executes a 1-touch return pass to A) or staying where he is (in which case A calls out "turn" and C receives ball, turns and passes it to C. Repeat other direction. Rotate position every 10 recep- tions.*

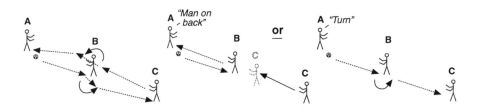

A

B

C

A "Man on back"

B

or

C

A "Turn"

B

C

B

. <u>**Water Break**</u> (5 min.)

During water break set up grid for IVA below.

IV. Large Group Activity

A. <u>**Full Team Scrimmage**</u> (12 min.)

Divide players into 2 equal teams and play regulation scrimmage. Use throw-ins, goal and corner kicks. Do not stop play but encourage proper positions and excel- lent ball control. Tell players: "Don't Panic." "Take your time and do the right thing with the ball."

End

Beginning of
Practice
Field Set-up
(50 yds. x
100 yds.)

10 yd,
squares

Session 16

<table>
<tr><td>Start
Times</td><td></td><td>Coaching
Keys</td></tr>
</table>

Start Times

I. Warm Ups

Coaching Keys

__:___ **A. Team Keep Away** (5 min.)

Divide players into 2 equal teams with colored bibs. On a large grid 1/3 to 1/2 of a regulation field, play keep away with each team trying to score points by making 3 (or 4, 5, etc.) consecutive passes without opponents touching the ball. Coach counts passes out loud and calls out score.

☞ *Winning team gets butts-up penalty shot at losers from 15 yards away.*

__:___ **B. Dribble Around Outside of Field** (5 min.)

Each player with a ball dribbles ball around outside edge of regulation field.

__:___ **C. Four-Sided Shooting Game** (5 min.)

One or two grids 10 yds. square with one 4' wide cone goal centered on each side of square, 6-15 players per grid. Put 2 equal teams (with colored bibs) in each grid. Score as many goals as possible in any goal. Coach throws in new ball, and calls out score, every time a goal is scored or ball leaves the grid.

10 yd. sq. grid

Coach   Coach

☞ *Coach keep balls coming fast. Lob some for header shots. Praise aggressive play.*

__:___ **D. Water Break** (5 min.)

During water break set up cones for IIA & IIB below.

II. Individual Skill Activities

(Theme: Set Play Tactics)

__:___ **A. Throw-In Practice--Pairs** (5 min.)

Divide players into pairs, each pair with 1 ball. Begin drill at one corner of field. Player A1 executes a throw-in on ground leading A2 as A2 sprints past A1. A2 dribbles ball to next cone on side-line and does a throw-in to A1 as A1 sprints past A2, and so on, all the way around outside of field. B1 and B2 begin as soon as A2 makes his throw in from the second cone.

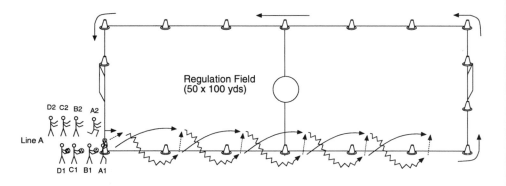

Regulation Field
(50 x 100 yds)

D2 C2 B2 A2

Line A

D1 C1 B1 A1

__:___ **B. Throw-In Tactics--Rear and Front Support** **(10 min.)**

Three single file lines as shown on diagram. "Fielder with the ball" (A) takes throw-in. He has option of throwing to "Fielder B," who is making a "front support run", or to "Fielder C" providing rear support.

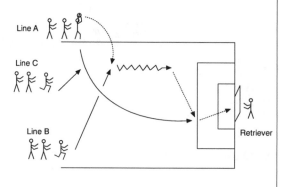

__:___ **Throw-In to B** **(5 min.)**

After receiving throw-in, B dribbles to corner and centers ball for a shot by A who has run behind B to center. C provides rear support for B.

__:___ **Throw-In to C** **(5 min.)**

C receives throw-in from A. After his run past A, B circles back for cross pass from C. B executes a 1-touch pass back to A who has timed a front support run for a shot. Practice one play at a time but use all three positions. Players rotate from Line A to B to C to A.

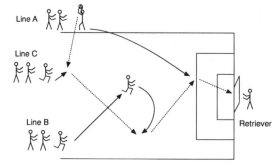

__:___ **C. Water Break** **(5 min.)**

During water break set up grids for IVA below.

III. Small Group Activity

(None)

IV. Large Group Activity

__:___ **A. 3 vs. 3 Scrimmage** **(10 min.)**

Divide players into 3-man teams. Use as many 20 x 30 yd. grids as are necessary to accommodate all players at same time. Scrimmage 3 vs. 3 emphasizing positions, rear and front support on both set plays and regular field play, minimum 10 yds. between players. Use your own field size and rules if involved in a 3-sided soccer league.

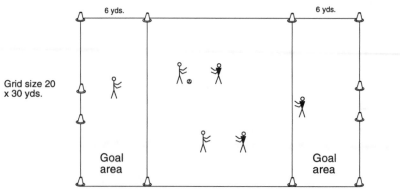

__:___ **End**

Beginning of Practice Field Set-up
20 - 50 yds.
30 - 60 yds.

Session 17

(vertical text) Tear out along perforation.

Start Times

I. Warm Ups

Coaching Keys

__:___ **A. Brazilian Jog (5 min.)**

Two single file lines standing side by side. Players "jog" wherever the front 2 players lead them for 5 minutes. As they jog, the coach (or front 2 players) calls out "right hand" and all players touch ground with "right hand," "left hand," both hands, header jumps, skip, front roll etc. and the player's respond.

__:___ **B. 1 vs. 1 Dribbling and Shooting (10 min.)**

Set up 2 practice stations as shown in diagram with 6-9 players per station. At each station form two single file lines near far end of grid and one line of defenders next to goal post. Coach (or defenders) alternates kicking ball to A1 or B1. D1 leaves as ball is kicked and runs forward to defend. A1 (or B1) tries to dribble past D1 and score goal. If D1 successfully steals ball, he tries to dribble ball through one of cone goals near side-line while A1 tries to recover ball. Offensive player rotates to defense line and defender rotates to line A or B.

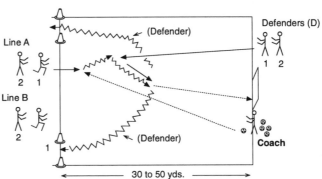

II. Individual Skill Activity

(Theme: Combination)

__:___ **A. Read the Defender Drill (15 min.)**

Set up 2 practice stations as shown in diagram with 6-9 players per station. At each station form lines A, B and C as shown in diagram with coach or player acting as server and 1 or 2 retrievers. Lines A and B are offensive players and line C are defenders. As coach kicks ball to A player, defender sprints forward to defend. A must make a good reception of the ball and also decide whether to pass to B (who advances slowly down left side for a pass), or to try to dribble past C for the shot. Decision will depend upon what C does on defense. A must make correct decision. If ball is passed to B, B shoots and A makes forward support run in case B is covered by C. Rotate sides. Also add a second defender after 10 minutes. Coach keeps track of good "receptions" by A, good "passes to B," shots, correct decisions, etc.

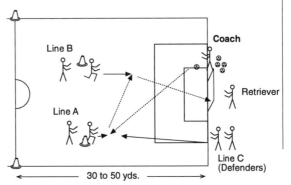

__:__ **B.** <u>Water Break</u> (5 min.)

__:__ **C.** <u>2 vs. 1 Dribble and Shooting</u> (10 min.)
Same set up as IB above except A1 and B1 play together against D1. Call for wall passes and keep minimum 10 yds. between players.

III. Small Group Activity

(None)

IV. Large Group Activity

__:__ **A.** <u>Full Team Scrimmage</u> (15 min.)
Divide players into 2 equal teams and play regulation scrimmage. Use throw-ins, goal and corner kicks. Encourage calm ball control and decision-making, always finding the open man.

__:__ **End**

Beginning of
Practice
Field Set-up
(25 yds. x
40 yds.;
Goals = 5 yds.)

IA.

25 yds.

40 yds.

Session 18

I. Warm Ups

Tear out along perforation.

__:__ **A. Dribbling Jingle Jangle Races** (8 min.)

Divide players into 3-man teams and line them up as shown in diagram. Race begins on coach's whistle. One player at a time on each team dribbles ball around first cone and back to start. Then each player on the team dribbles around second cone and back to start. Then each player dribbles around third cone and back to start. First team finished wins. Run several races.

__:__ **B. Ball Touch Drill** (2 min.)

All players stand with ball on ground between feet. Hop from 1 foot to the other touching top of ball lightly with bottom of foot that is off the ground. Go for speed.

__:__ **C. 3 vs. 3 vs. 3 Scrimmage** (15 min.)

Divide players into 3-man teams and give each team a different color bib. Place three, 3-man teams, on a grid 25 x 40 yds. as shown in diagram. Team in middle (Team B) begins with ball and attacks Team A. If B scores a goal, they keep ball (new ball) and attack Team C going the other direction. If A gains possession vs. B, B can try to regain possession until Team A crosses mid-field line, but if unsuccessful A attacks C under same rules. If you have more than 3 teams, have extra players run a circle passing drill beside the grid and substitute them into the scrimmage every 5 minutes. If you have less than 9 players, use a 2 vs. 2 vs. 2 format.

Grid 25yds. x 40 yds.

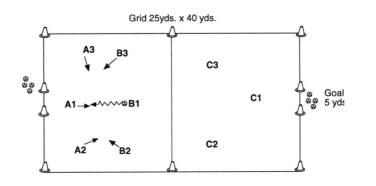

__:__ **D. Water Break** (5 min.)

During water break set up cones for IIA below.

II. Individual Skill Activity

(Theme: Defense)

__:___ **A. Progressive Defensive Tactics Drill**   (15 min.)

Set up 2 or more practice stations as shown in diagram; 5-7 players per station. At each station form one line of defenders and one line of offensive players as shown. First stage: offensive player O tries to run (without ball) past defender D without making body contact. D tries to stop O, or force O out the side of the lane, by gaining and maintaining "goal-side position." Players rotate after every turn and run both positions 2 times.   Second stage: Same as first stage except O has ball. D may not tackle the ball. He just tries to stop O's advance with good goal-side position. Third stage: D may now tackle the ball and body contact is allowed. Fourth stage: Widen lane to 8 to 10 yds. (continue to allow tackling and body contact).

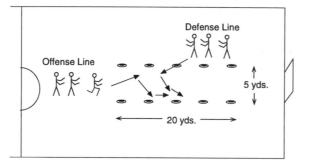

__:___ **B. Water Break**   (5 min.)

During water break set up grids for IVA below.

III. Small Group Activity

(None)

IV. Large Group Activity

__:___ **A. 3 vs. 3 Scrimmage**   (10 min.)

Divide players into 3-man teams. Use as many 20 x 30 yd. grids as are necessary to accommodate all players at the same time. Scrimmage 3 vs. 3 emphasizing good defensive position (i.e. goal-side) and tackling techniques. Use your own field size and rules if involved in a 3-sided soccer league.

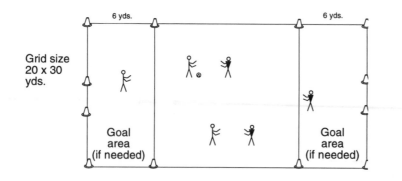

__:___ **End**

Start Times

Tear out along perforation.

I. Warm Ups

__:___ **A. Pairs Passing Moving** (5 min.)

Pairs 8 yds. apart. Pass ball back and forth while running length of field. "Control" ball on every reception using 2 or more touches. Accurate passes with good touch. "Lead" your partner.

__:___ **B. Cross, Control and Shoot** (10 min.)

Set up 1 or 2 practice stations, minimum 7 players per station. At each station form two lines of players as shown in diagram. Coach acts as passive defender. Line A players dribble a few yards into penalty area. As defender (coach) moves toward them they "cross" the ball to the Line B player. B player uses a 2-touch reception and shot. Players rotate from Lines A and B to retriever and then to opposite lines. Run drill from both sides.

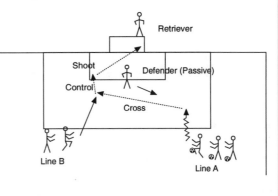

II. Individual Skill Activities

(Theme: Passing)

__:___ **A. 3-Man Weave** (10 min.)

Three single file lines at mid-field line. A1 begins with ball and passes to B1 who is running diagonally toward the middle of field. A1 runs behind and around B1 (the person he passed to) and curves back toward middle. B1 receives the pass from A1 and passes to C1 who has run down field and curved to middle ready to receive pass. B1 runs behind and around C1 and curves back toward middle. C1 receives the pass from B1, passes to A1, and runs behind and around A1 and curves back toward the middle, and so on. Limit touches to 4, 3 then 2. Run drill both directions using a cone goal at mid-field line or other end.

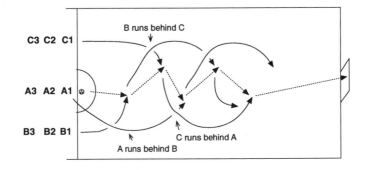

__:___ **B. Water Break** (5 min.)

During water break set up grids for IIIA below.

__:___   **C.**   <u>**Wall Pass Drill**</u>   **(10 min.)**

Set up 2 practice stations; 6-7 players per station. Position the players as shown in diagram. A runs down middle of the row of players executing wall passes (i.e. give and go passes) with players B, C and D. Players B, C and D must use a soft con-

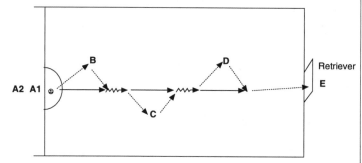

trolled "1-touch" return pass to A. After last wall pass from D, A shoots a goal. Players rotate from E to D to C to B to end of line A. Players B, C and D run behind A to their new position, immediately after making their wall pass to A.

III.   Small Group Activity

__:___   **A.**   <u>**Zone Scrimmage 3 vs. 3**</u>   **(15 min.)**

Set up 20 x 30 yd. grids as shown in diagram, 6 players per grid with enough grids to accommodate all players at the same time. Scrimmage A Team vs. B Team. Players A1 and B1 must stay between sideline and cones as must players A3 and B3 on other side. Players A2 and B2 must stay in middle zone. Require at least 2 passes to wings, or 1 pass to each wing, before a shot may be taken.

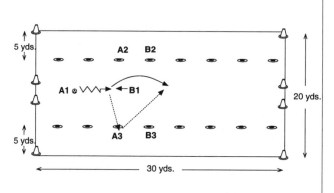

IV.   Large Group Activity

__:___   **A.**   <u>**Running Relay Races**</u>   **(5 min.)**

Divide players into 2 or more relay teams; 3-4 players per team. Each player must run, weaving through the cones, for 20 yds. carrying a ball. He sets ball down in cone square and continues running another 20 yds. to end of cones. There he does a forward roll and then weaves back through the cones, picks up ball at midway point, and weaves through remaining cones to "hand" ball to next teammate.

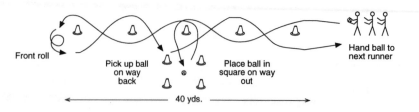

__:___   **End**

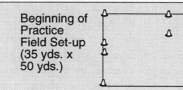

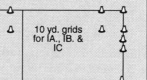

Start Times		Coaching Keys

I. Warm Ups

__:___ **A. <u>Confined Area Dribbling</u>** (5 min.)

All players in small grids, e.g., 8 to 10 players in 10 x 10 yd. grid. One ball per player. Dribble ball around in grid. No collisions. Coach calls out--fast, slow, medium, right turn, left, reverse, etc.

10 yd. sq. grid

__:___ **B. <u>Confined Area Passing</u>** (5 min.)

Same grid as IA. Divide players into pairs, one ball per pair. Pass ball back and forth while moving around grid. Pass and move, pass and move, etc. throughout grid. No collisions with balls or other players.

10 yd. sq. grid

__:___ **C. <u>Scatter Game</u>** (5 min.)

Same grid as IA and IB. One ball per player. Try to kick other players' balls out of square and protect your own. Use 10 second count down for last 2 players to determine a winner.

__:___ **D. <u>Team Keep Away</u>** (5 min.)

Divide players into 2 equal teams with colored bibs. On a large grid 1/3 to 1/2 of a regulation field, play keep away with each team trying to score points by making 3 (4, 5, etc.) consecutive passes without opponents touching the ball. Coach counts passes out loud and calls out score.

☞ *Award the winners a butts-up penalty shot at losers from 15 yards away.*

__:___ **E. <u>Water Break</u>** (5 min.)

During water break set up grids for IIA below.

II. Individual Skill Activities

(Theme: All Skills)

__:___ **A. <u>1 vs. 1 Scrimmage</u>** (10 min.)

Set up as many 20 x 25 yd. grids as are necessary to accommodate all players at same time with 4 players per grid. Two players act as goalies while other 2 scrimmage 1 vs. 1. Goalies keep supply of balls near goal.

On "saves" goalie distributes ball to player defending that goalie's goal and any time ball leaves grid, the goalie in that half of grid quickly throws in a new ball anywhere on that 1/2 of grid. Each pair plays 2 minutes, then switches with other pair. Emphasize dribbling (fakes, feints, etc.) and shooting on offense and quick recovery of "goal-side position" on transition to defense.

__:__ **B. Water Break** (5 min.)

During water break, set up grids for IVA below.

III. Small Group Activity
(None)

IV. Large Group Activity

__:__ **A. 3 vs. 3 Scrimmage** (10 min.)

Divide players into 3-man teams. Use as many 20 x 30 yd. grids as are necessary to accommodate all players at the same time. Scrimmage 3 vs. 3 emphasizing calm, patient ball control, position responsibilities and good decision-making. Minimum 10 yds. between players and rear and front support.

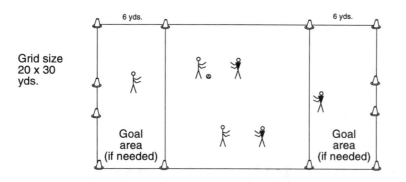

__:__ **B. Team Discussion** (5 min.)

End of season. Thank players for great effort at learning how to play soccer and for being good friends and teammates to one another. Everyone take pride in the upcoming last game in your individual skills, decision-making and condition and try your hardest to win.

__:__ **End**

Commentaries
To
Practice Sessions

Following is a set of 20 Commentaries for the Polumbus Practice Sessions . There is one Commentary for each of the 20 Practice Sessions.

Each Commentary is designed to supplement and expand upon the contents of the Practice Session with which it is associated and to provide some helpful hints on how to coach the specific skills, drills, games and competitions set forth in the Daily Practice Session. It should take no more than 20 minutes to read and understand each Commentary.

COMMENTARY

General Atmosphere

The most important thing you can accomplish in the first four practice sessions is to create a positve atmosphere with no pressure and to display a caring love for the kids. They will have a natural anxiety about how tough, mean or demanding you are going to be as a coach. They will sense your true intentions not only from what you say, but from the expression on your face (smile), from your tone of voice, your patience, the strictness with which you run your practice and your tendency to focus on the positives or the negatives. Laugh, touch them and hug them often. Discipline childish behavior very lightly if at all for several weeks. Just have unabashed fun so they firmly associate soccer with fun!

Practice Activities

This practice session is designed primarily for you to gather information about your players' abilities and to introduce the kids to the game. Note which foot is dominant, how they kick the ball (off toe, instep, etc.) and their overall athletic ability. Encourage them to kick their hardest in the kicking contest and to run their fastest in the foot race and agility course and to score the most points in the accuracy shooting drill (i.e., encourage competitive aspects). But do not coach them on how to do any of it. Once you explain and demonstrate each activity, do not correct the kids. Just let it happen. The scrimmage has no purpose except to get the ball and try to kick it in the goal and to have fun.

For teams in their third to fourth season, you may want to replace the agility contest with a test of the players' basic skills.

I. Warm Ups

A. Kick and Chase.

For a practice session or two, try to avoid coaching and use this drill as an "energy release" for the kids. It is fun. They can run and they can kick the ball as hard as they want. Gently coax them to go as straight down the field as possible and slowly work in right foot only, both feet and possibly left foot (or non-dominant foot) to begin "technical" kicking and dribbling improvements.

B. Over and Under Relay.

Just for fun and ball touching experience.

C. Confined Area Dribbling.

This drill, and variations of it, you will use for years to come. It is an excellent drill for touching the ball, ball control and ball protection, close quarters dribbling and even physical conditioning. For now, leave it as a fun experience for the kids in trying not to crash their expensive cars, or to make their parents angry, cause insurance rates to increase, etc.

II. Individual Skill Activities

A. Kicking Demonstration.

1. General.
Kicking is an extremely important fundamental skill for the players to develop. Do not overlook it or underestimate its importance as many coaches have in the past. Many repetitions of each type of kick are necessary with the goal being that each child automatically uses them all with proper technique at the proper times for the proper purposes.

2. Most Common Error.
Almost all of your players will at first kick off the toe of their shoe as they have done on the playgrounds and at school in kick ball. Make a continuing effort to discourage this practice since it is a habit hard to break for most kids and it is an unreliable and inaccurate style of kicking.

3. Proper Technique for a Kick.
Regardless of the type of kick used, there is a general technique that is appropriate for all kicks:

   a. Step with Non-Kicking Foot. Players should be taught to always step forward with their non-kicking foot and plant it firmly 6 to 9 inches directly beside the center of ball (or, if moving, where the ball will be at the time it is kicked) with the toe of the non-kicking foot pointing directly at the target. The step insures movement of the entire body forward in good balance, which is important to the development of both accuracy and power in a kick. It is important to teach the players to try to never kick a ball without the step or while standing stationary on the non-kicking foot, swinging the kicking foot under their body. Demonstrate the absence of power in the wrong way as well as the power and accuracy accomplished in the right way.

   b. Eyes on the Ball. Instruct players to look before initiating the kick to see where to kick, but to always be looking at the ball at the time the kick is made.

   c. Follow Through. On a typical inside foot kick, it is important to bend at the waist and follow through high with the leg swinging towards the target while maintaining good balance.

4. Three Types of Kicks.

   a. Inside-of-Foot. Utilizing the proper steps and follow-through described above, and keeping the eyes on the ball, the player makes ball contact with the inside of the foot in the arch area. The foot strikes the middle of the ball. Player must hold his toe up and heel down and the foot must be turned out at right angles to the target line. Best use is for short accurate passes. It is also good for quick release situations. Medium range power can and should be developed.

    b. <u>Outside-of-Foot</u>. This is an extremely valuable type of kick for quick release on passes or shots and for dribbling feints and short pass situations in crowded areas. An amazing amount of power can be developed with this type of kick although this is not its primary purpose or value. In this type of kick the ball is contacted with the outside of the foot from the arch forward and pushed to the side at an angle from the direction the player is running.

    c. <u>Instep or Shoelaces ("Power Kick").</u> In this type of kick, the toe is pointed down toward the ground and the ball is contacted with the shoelaces or the top of the foot. For a high trajectory long pass or shot the foot is swung around slightly more on the side of the body to keep the toe from dragging the ground and the foot strikes the lower half of the ball. The player leans back at the moment of impact.

B.   **<u>Stationary Pairs Kicking.</u>**

During the pairs kicking drill make sure the kids are aware of how they are kicking the ball and encourage good balance and proper execution. At this stage learning the proper step with the non-kicking foot is more important than learning the actual techniques involved in each of the different types of kicks. Remember they will need many more repetitions than can be given in just this practice before you will see improvement.

III. Small Group Activity

A.   **<u>2 vs. 1 Scrimmage.</u>**

Scrimmaging with uneven teams (i.e. 2 vs. 1) encourages passing on the team with the most players. This will provide an excellent opportunity for the 2 players to practice good "technique" in their kicking, passing and shooting.

The player who is playing alone must play aggressive and intense defense and must use his or her dribbling skills to get past the 2 opponents. Because this player will wear down quickly, be sure to rotate the players every 1-2 minutes.

IV. Large Group Activity

A.   **<u>Full Team Scrimmage.</u>**

Be sure to send players to specific positions before starting the scrimmage and call the positions by name (i.e., forwards if in attack position, fullbacks if in a defense position and halfback or mid-fielder if in between). If playing 3 vs. 3 remind the kids that there should always be a "fielder with the ball" and a "front support fielder" and "rear support fielder." If your league uses a goalie in 3 vs. 3 soccer, have a keeper/sweeper and 2 fielders, one with the ball and one front support fielder. The keeper/sweeper provides rear support. The fielder with the ball tries to advance the ball forward by dribbling or passing it to the front support fielder and, if unable to do so, passes the ball back to his rear support.

This will begin the process of identification of positions and the notion of positional responsibility. Once the scrimmage has started, forget positions and let the kids run all over the field chasing the ball in groups. The purpose of today's scrimmage is to apply, in a game situation, the "kicking techniques" that the kids just learned. Encourage good kicking technique.

COMMENTARY

Session 3

I. Warm Ups

A. <u>**Kick and Chase.**</u>

Limit coaching. Have fun. Energy release. Coax them as straight down the field as possible. Try right foot only, left foot only and both feet.

B. <u>**Confined Area Dribbling.**</u>

Keys. Ball close to feet. Eyes up. Watch out for wrecks. Stay under control. Use both feet.

C. <u>**Scatter Game.**</u>

Limit coaching, but begin to use key phrases such as "protect your ball," "know where everyone is" before you leave your ball to kick someone else's out of square.

D. <u>**Two-Touch Passing Drill.**</u>

1. Demonstrate and Explain Technique.

    a. <u>First touch of ball is the most important touch in soccer.</u> It gives player "control" of the ball for passing, shooting or dribbling. It relieves pressure from defense. It sets up powerful kicking position. It builds confidence in the player.

    b. <u>Purpose of First Touch.</u> To lightly push ball 3 to 4 feet away and slightly to the side of the receiver into an open area. The open area will normally be in a direction away from the nearest defender. The 3 to 4 feet distance allows for a good step to be taken with the non-kicking foot in a follow-up kick without having to back up or adjust the body in order to execute the kicking motion. Demonstrate.

    c. <u>Keys.</u>

        (1) Soft touch with receiving foot held off the ground. (Use inside or outside of foot). Demonstrate.

        (2) Lay ball out the 3 to 4 feet away from your body in a perfect position for "kicking." Demonstrate where the perfect placement is by simply placing the ball there.

        (3) Step immediately to the ball after the first touch and either shoot, pass or begin dribbling. Demonstrate.

    d. <u>Interesting Note.</u> "Dribbling" is really just a series of first touches while moving down the field.

II. Individual Skill Activities

A.&B. <u>**Dribbling Drills.**</u>

Be sure to avoid long lines in these drills (see Diagrams) and keep the kids moving. Again, do not coach very much! It is a necessary step in learning for the kids to experience loss of control of the ball and the inability to make quick turns or turnarounds, etc. They will not listen to your "solution" if they do not realize they have a "problem."

After letting the kids go through the dribbling drills, lots of times begin to suggest that they are going to have to consider running only as fast as they can run while still "controlling" the ball. The object of soccer is to "control" the ball and keep it away from opponents. If you lose "control" opponents will get the ball.

III. Small Group Activities

A. <u>**1 vs. 1 Scrimmage.**</u>

Purpose of the 1 vs. 1 scrimmage is to insure lots of dribbling for all players. Try to make the kids conscious of "controlling" the ball while they dribble. It is just as important to "keep the ball" away from your opponent as it is to score a goal.

IV. Large Group Activity

A. <u>**Full Team Scrimmage.**</u>

To begin the scrimmage, give each player a specific position (even if playing less than 11-sided soccer) and call the position by its name. Keep communicating "position names" for familiarity but do not worry yet about responsibilities. Again, let the scrimmage itself be the coach. It will provide all of the game type situations needed for learning. Occasionally blow your whistle and stop play and remind the kids to dribble well and to try not to lose the ball before they pass or shoot.

I. Warm Ups

A. **<u>Wheel Barrow Nudge Race.</u>**

Just for fun.

B. **<u>Two-Touch Passing Drill.</u>**

Key is "good demonstration" showing (1) a perfect "first touch" leaving the ball one full step in front and slightly to one side of the player; (2) an immediate step to the ball with non-kicking foot properly planted beside ball and (3) the second touch pass back to partner with good touch and control. Coach counts "out loud" with a consistent rhythm or cadence (e.g., one pause two...one pause two...one pause two) during the demonstration and then, does the same for each child as he walks around during the drill.

C. **<u>Throw-In Practice.</u>**

Be strict on technique after players have made a few throw-ins and are continuing to use improper technique. Practice easy and hard throw-ins to be sure feet stay on ground when throwing hard.

II. Individual Skill Activity
(Theme: Shooting)

A. **<u>Triple-Shot Drill.</u>**

If done properly, this drill will develop good shooting technique, use of both feet for shooting and quickness and aggressiveness during shooting opportunities. It is also good for agility and physical conditioning. Emphasize: (1) "When ball is in area in front of goal" it is shooting time; (2) shoot ball hard; (3) plant non-kicking foot hard in proper location next to ball. (4) kick ball on instep (i.e., shoelaces) for most powerful shot (Note: If too difficult for some kids, use inside of foot as alternative); (4) react immediately after shooting one ball to turn around and run as fast as you can back around cone for next shot; (5) use right foot on right side-left foot on left side and choice for third shot from the middle.

III. Small Group Activity

A.&B. **<u>2 vs. 2 Rapid Shooting Drill and Four-Sided Shooting Game.</u>**

Again, limit coaching and avoid "technique" emphasis. These games are extremely fun and fast moving and are designed to develop quick and aggressive reactions to shooting opportunities. Coach puts new ball in play quickly after every shot or ball out-of-bounds and calls out score every time a new ball is put in play. Occasionally, during the four-sided shooting game, require "one pass" before a shot. Be sure to determine the winning team.

IV. Large Group Activity

A. **<u>Discussion of Triangles.</u>**

Your young players may not even know what a triangle looks like or that they come in many shapes and sizes. With pictures or drawings, **show the kids the shapes of many triangles** that are formed by three players (each player being a corner of a triangle.)

Explain that **the objective of the players is to always have one point of the triangle (i.e., one player) behind the "player with the ball" providing "rear support" and one point of the triangle (i.e., another player) in front of the "player with the ball" providing "front support."** All three players change position after every pass (and sometimes while one player is dribbling).

The player providing "front support" is called the "**front support fielder**." His primary offensive responsibility (while in this position) is to make penetrating runs in front of the "fielder with the ball" trying to get open for a pass and/or shot on goal.

The player providing "rear support" is called the "**rear support fielder**." His primary responsibility (while in this position) is to provide rear support on the attack and to provide defense and protect the goal in the event of a ball turnover.

The player with the ball is called the "**fielder with the ball**" and his primary offensive responsibility is to penetrate the defense of the opponents by dribbling or passing to the front support fielder. Whenever forward movement is prevented by the defense, he may make back passes to the rear support fielder allowing the player in rear support to initiate a new attack.

If your league plays 3 vs. 3 soccer **with a goalie**, the player providing "rear support" is called the "sweeper" or "keeper/sweeper" and he should **not** change positions during play. In addition to providing rear support on offense, this player has primary responsibility for protecting the goal and playing defense.

The players should be told that the shape of the triangle is not important. Any shape is okay as long as it is a triangle. The only thing the players need to remember to be in a good formation is to stay a **minimum of 10 yards apart** (i.e., the sides of the triangle must be at least 10 yds. long).

All players must **transcend quickly and aggressively from offense to defense** whenever opponents get the ball. They must (1) get back fast; (2) gain and maintain goal-side position on the ball and opponents and (3) aggressively tackle the ball.

3 vs. 3 Scrimmage. In today's 3 vs. 3 scrimmage emphasize positions, playing responsibilities and minimum 10 yds. between players on offense. Do not, however, stop the scrimmage to coach. Encourage lots of shooting since that is the theme of today's practice.

COMMENTARY

Session 5

I. Warm Ups

A. **<u>Body Parts Game.</u>**

Good for fun, balance and agility.

B. **<u>Dribbling and Reaction Drill.</u>**

Vary length of periods between whistles. Smile and challenge the kids.

C. **<u>Keep Away.</u>**

Explain purpose is to keep ball away from defender as long as possible. Let the kids play for a while without any instruction. They will bunch up chasing the ball. Stop play and tell 3 offensive players they must stay within 3 feet of a sideline, and even though they should move and change positions, there is only one player at a time allowed on each side-line (ie., "spread out"). Again, do not coach, but let the game teach the kids. Near end of drill begin dropping key words and phrases such as "stay spread out," "get open," and "support" your teammate when he is in trouble. "Move" to "open space or area" without the ball.

II. Individual Skill Activities
(Theme: Passing)

A. **<u>Confined Area Passing.</u>**

You will be amazed at how naturally your offensive players will "spread out" and "back up" to receive a hand held pass of the ball over the head of the defender in the first part of this keep away drill. It will be a disaster of equal proportions when you put the ball on the ground and play keep away with the feet (kicking). When you go back to "hands keep away" begin to point out to the players how they are moving to get "open" in a direction away from the ball or away from the players who have the ball." Explain that this is also necessary to do when passing with the feet. Go back and forth from hands to feet.

III. Small Group Activity

A. **<u>One Touch Passing Drill.</u>**

Sometimes during a soccer game there is not enough time for a player to use the first touch of the ball to bring it under control before he dribbles, shoots or passes. His first touch must be a "pass" or "shot," and the ball is usually moving before he touches it.

In this circle drill, you will be practicing short controlled 1-touch passing that requires excellent touch and aim. Players should use only the inside of foot pass in this drill. The key to coaching is to be sure players have their "eyes-on-the-ball" at impact. To encourage eyes-on-the-ball instruct players to "see" their foot strike the "middle of the ball" (i.e., not too high or too low on the back of the ball.)

IV. Large Group Activity

A. **<u>Full Team Scrimmage.</u>**

Young players get frustrated easily in a game-type situation when they are restricted in any way from running up and down the field and kicking the ball as hard as they can. To avoid boredom and frustration, be sure to limit the time you scrimmage under the restrictions of a limited number of touches or a minimum number of passes before a shot can be taken. Be sure to give them plenty of time near the end of the scrimmage, for unrestricted play. Do not miss the opportunity, if using 3 vs. 3 scrimmage, to teach the actual concepts of rear and front support and the need for the players without the ball to "move without the ball," to a location to provide the "support" they are responsible for.

COMMENTARY

Session 6

I. Warm Ups

A. Ball Touch Drill.

This is a great ball touching and physical conditioning activity. At first it is difficult for some young kids to do, but they feel good when they master it. Use this often just for fun and see who can do it the fastest. Develops "quick feet." Key: Be sure kids balance themselves and put 100 percent of their weight on the foot that is on the ground. They should not try to support themselves with the foot that is used to touch the ball.

B. Ball Hop.

Good agility and physical conditioning drill. It is extra fun for the kids to face the coach at one end of a single file line and copy the coach's jumps over the ball. Coach uses bursts of 1 jump, 3 jumps, 10 jumps, etc. and sometimes very slow or very fast.

C. Four-Sided Shooting Game.

It is always wise to develop a hunger for goals in the players. This is also a good conditioning game and is excellent for developing "aggressiveness" in your players.

II. Individual Skill Activities

A. Goal-side Position Drill Without Ball.

The first time you try this drill, there will be many defensive players who seem to have their feet stuck in cement and the more aggressive players will win every challenge. Narrow the lane if the offense is winning too easily. You want the defense to experience what success is really like in maintaining goal-side position. Also match players of equal aggressiveness and/or equal physical ability.

This is also a great drill for the offensive players to develop fakes, feints or moves to get around the defender. Encourage "jukes" and "shuks and jives" and praise every effort no matter how bad it looks.

Key word for coaching this drill is "position." Play defense by keeping good "position." Never give up "goalside position" even when tackling the ball.

B. Goal-side Position Drill With Ball.

Emphasize to the defensive players that maintaining "goal-side position" is the first objective of the defense. Tackling (stealing) the ball and clearing the ball to the sidelines are secondary objectives. This drill offers good close-quarters dribbling and shooting practice for the offensive player.

III. Small Group Activity

A. 2 vs. 2 Small-Sided Scrimmage.

The purpose of the narrow field is to encourage success in maintaining goal-side position. This scrimmage is an extension of the Goal-side Position Drill to a game-like atmosphere. Use the word "position" often.

IV. Large Group Activity

A. Full Team Scrimmage.

Watch for opportunities to complement defensive players when keeping good goal-side position. Call out "position, position, position" during appropriate moments of scrimmage. If your team plays 3 vs. 3 games in its league and you are using 3 vs. 3 in this drill, be sure to continue to emphasize position responsibilities and front and rear support roles.

COMMENTARY

I. Warm Ups

A. Running and Reaction Drill.

Have fun! Keep kids guessing by whistling without any rhythm or cadence and by using a variety of calls. Example: few reverses at first, then maybe 2 fairly quick ones; then maybe 4 quick reverses in a row. Use for physical fitness and agility training as well as for reaction and training in decision-making.

B. Two-Touch Passing Drill.

1. Demonstrate.

   a. <u>First touch of a ball is the most important touch in soccer.</u> It gives player "control" of the ball for passing, shooting or dribbling. It relieves pressure from defense. It sets up powerful kicking position. It builds confidence in the player.

   b. <u>Purpose of first touch.</u> To lightly push ball 3 to 4 feet away and slightly to the side of the receiver into an open area. The open area will normally be in a direction away from the nearest defender. The 3 to 4 feet distance allows for a good step to be taken with the non-kicking foot in a follow-up kick without having to back up or adjust the body in order to execute the kicking motion.

   c. <u>Keys:</u>

   (1) Soft touch with receiving foot held off the ground. (Use inside or outside of foot.)

   (2) Lay ball out 3 to 4 feet away from your body in a perfect position for "kicking."

   (3) Step immediately to the ball after the first touch and either shoot, pass or begin dribbling.

   d. <u>Interesting note.</u> "Dribbling" is really just a series of first touches while moving down the field.

C. Ball Touch and Juggling.

The ball touch drill is very physically demanding. Be sure not to ruin the fun of this drill by letting the kids over do it. Intermingling some activity such as the "ball throw with feet" keeps it fun. This will introduce the concept of ball juggling which the kids perceive as "fancy" and "fun" and the coach perceives as excellent "ball control" training.

II. Individual Skill Activities
(Theme: Shielding)

A. Ball Shielding Drill.

The "first touch" by the receiver/shielder is critical. The player must use the first touch to move the ball to a position that will allow the player to move between the ball and the defender quickly. Encourage fair but aggressive play by both players being sure they understand that shoulder to shoulder physical contact is both legal and appropriate. Coach "body position," "balance and quick feet," "lots of quick, soft touches of the ball," and a "poised" but "aggressive" determination to keep the ball. (See Commentary for Daily Practice Session Eight, Paragraph IIA.)

III. Small Group Activity

A. One on One Ball Possession.

This drill is similar to the Ball Shielding drill in paragraph IIB above but is much more competitive. It is also much more physically demanding. Give the players plenty of breaks and half way through the drill change partners in all the squares.

IV. Large Group Activity

A. Narrow Field Scrimmage.

The purpose of the narrow field is to create congestion and opportunities for ball shielding. Have a contest to see who can keep the ball the longest and still make a good pass or shot.

COMMENTARY

I. Warm Ups

A. **Brazilian Jog.**

Made famous by the Brazilian National Soccer Team, use your creativity to come up with any type of "calls" you want. Main value of drill is aerobic, so keep them running for the full time period. The "calls" are just for fun.

B. **Receive and React.**

Discipline is important. Players must actually "shuffle feet" (i.e., not cross them) while moving back and forth from cone to cone. Ball should arrive at each cone just as the player arrives. Encourage a "perfect first touch" to emphasize the importance of "collecting" and "controlling" the ball first, before passing it back. After return pass, the player must initiate his shuffle back to the other cone "immediately." Pace should be steady and quick but not break-neck speed.

C. **Serve and Defend.**

Defender must be very aggressive, but must allow offensive player ample time to "receive and control" the ball before "closing" on him. Offensive player must dribble and fake as well as shield and protect the ball while trying to get a shot.

II. Individual Skill Activity
(Theme: Receiving and Ball Shielding)

A. **Ball Shielding Demonstration.**

With players sitting with back to sun, discuss the fact that "ball shielding" is a very aggressive and physical activity. While shielding or protecting a ball, the player must have sufficient strength, skills and poise to physically battle an aggressive opponent who is trying to steal the ball, while at the same time look over the playing field to determine what should be done with the ball and when to do it. The "shielder" cannot become so focused on the opponent that he cannot see the rest of the playing field and make good decisions.

The key to having this poise is to develop your shielding skills to the point where they happen by instinct and automatically when situations arise. When this occurs, the player will be able to see the "field" as well as his immediate opponent and will be able to focus his attention on doing the right thing with the ball.

Keys to Ball Shielding.

1. Body Position.
   a. between ball and opponent
   b. legs spread out
   c. facing sideways or at right angles to opponent and ball

2. Balance and Quick Feet.
   a. to maintain body position between ball and opponent
   b. to lean into opponent
   c. to push ball in desired direction
   d. to be ready to execute a strong, accurate pass when time is right

3. Soft Ball Touch.
   a. To move ball away from opponent

4. Aggressive Attitude.
   a. to fend off an aggressive opponent

5. *Poise and Concentration.*
   a. to avoid getting too "tied up" in the act of protecting the ball
   b. to be able to do something good with the ball at the right moment

Demonstrate above keys in semi-active conditions ending the "shielding" with a short pass to a teammate who "calls" for the ball (by calling out your name) as he runs by as if on a penetrating run to initiate an attack.

B.   **Ball Shielding Drill.**

The "first touch" by the receiver/shielder is critical. The player must use the first touch to move the ball to a position that will allow the player to move between the ball and the defender quickly. Encourage fair but aggressive play by both players being sure they understand that shoulder to shoulder physical contact is both legal and appropriate. Coach "body position," "balance and quick feet," "lots of short, soft touches of the ball," and a "poised" but "aggressive" determination to keep the ball.

III. Small Group Activity

A.   **1 vs. 1 Dribble Goal Game.**

Both players must play very aggressively on both offense and defense for this drill to maximize its value to the players. Encourage players to try hard and let them know up front they will have plenty of rest periods. Purpose of drill is to practice dribbling, ball shielding and ball control under competitive conditions.

IV. Large Group Activity

A.   **Full Team Scrimmage.**

It is important at this stage of the season for you to continue training your players to react to "restart" situations properly when the ball leaves the field of play. They should begin to understand that a throw-in will be used on side-line if ball crosses it and that a goal kick or corner kick will be used when ball crosses goal line. Discourage bunching up around the thrower or goal or corner kicker, but do not interrupt practice to show players their positions on these set plays. Do, however, encourage "position notions" and responsibilities of each position for defense, rear and front support, etc. Remind the players before the scrimmage and once (only once) near the middle of the scrimmage. Otherwise, let them play.

I. Warm Ups

A. **Ball Touch Drill.**

You know the drill by now! Make it fun. See how fast the kids can go. "Quick Feet.!"

B. **Ball Hop.**

Make it fun. Go for "height" in the jump over the ball. Then go for speed and agility.

C. **Jog Around Outside of Field.**

For aerobic purposes, not a race, but don't let anyone stop running until they have past the finish line.

D. **Circle Passing.**

During first part of drill focus on accurate, firm passes and good 2-touch receptions. Passers call out name of intended receiver. As you progress through the stages of the drill, try to keep players concentrating on the "changing conditions" in each phase. Make the last phase with defenders a challenge for the passers to make "perfect passes." Count out loud the number of consecutive passes the players make without the defenders touching the ball.

II. Individual Skill Activity
(Theme: Passing)

A. **Full Team Keep Away.**

This is an excellent game for physical conditioning. Make sure all players play hard by constantly counting out loud the number of consecutive passes by each team and the score of the game. If ball leaves field of play, throw new ball in on opposite side of field to spread players out and cause them to run.

Players should always focus on "perfect first touch," and good ball control in receiving passes. "Movement without the ball" is the critical factor, however, in successfully keeping the ball for a long series of passes. Players must always be moving to "get open" for a pass and to "support" their teammate with the ball. Occasionally, stop the game and remind the players of the importance of "supporting" to the "rear, forward and sides" of the player with the ball, giving the player lots of options to choose from.

B. **Water Break.**

C. **2 vs. 1 Scrimmages.**

Purpose of this drill today is to encourage lots of quick short passes by the team with 2 players. To avoid it becoming a "one pass and dribble" drill, it is important to limit the touches by the 2-man team to 2 or 3 touches. This will force the "passer" to make an "immediate" "forward support run" every time a pass is made, i.e., pass and move...pass and move.

The one-man team must emphasize dribbling skills and defensive position trying to maintain a "goalside position" on the ball at all times.

The drill is intentionally designed to create success for the passing 2-man team since they have a 2 on 1 advantage.

III. Small Group Activity
None

IV. Large Group Activity

A. 3 vs. 3 Scrimmage.

By this time in your practice, the players have been barraged with the concept of "supporting" the "player with the ball" in rear, front and side positions. Keep up the theme. 3 vs. 3 scrimmage is designed to provide front and rear support for the player with the ball utilizing the numerical advantage the triangle formation can create. To keep the scrimmages focused on passing, eliminate dribbling by limiting players to 2 or 3 touches.

COMMENTARY

I. Warm Ups

A. <u>Kick and Chase Races With Stop Whistle.</u>

Today you will use this drill more for "controlled dribbling" than for the uninhibited kicking and running purposes it has had in earlier practices. In order for the players to be able to stop quickly and trap the ball, it will be necessary for them to keep the ball close to their bodies while racing. Determine a "winner" each time you blow the whistle (i.e., the player who first has his ball successfully trapped under his foot) as well as a winner of every race.

B. <u>Jog Around Outside of Field.</u>

Stay in formation while jogging. It develops team pride. Not a race, but must be sure all players "run" the entire time and distance to insure the aerobic values of the drill.

C. <u>Round-the-Cones and Shoot.</u>

Insist on instep (or shoelace) kicks for the shots. Shoot hard and low at the corners of the net. Only "one-touch" shots so players must take shot "on-the-run" as the ball is "moving." Use "left foot" when circling around cones to the right and use "right foot" when circling around cones to the left. Be disciplined and do it right.

II. Individual Skill Activity
(Theme: Shooting)

A. <u>Continuous Shooting Drill.</u>

Again, be disciplined to use instep (shoelace) kicks, 1-touch shots and attempt to shoot hard and low in the corner of the net. Use right foot shots from line A and left foot shots from line B (but servers must be careful to "lead" the shooters as shown in diagram).

B. <u>Shooting vs. Defender.</u>

This is really the same drill as IIA except it adds the element of defensive pressure or a more game-like situation. Shooters use same techniques (i.e., 1-touch, instep kick, hard and low at corner of goal with proper foot) as in Drill IIA, but emphasize "poise" and "concentration" by the shooter. If defenders are successfully blocking shots, move their line farther away until shooters have sufficient time to get shot off.

III. Small Group Activity

A. <u>Center Goal Soccer.</u>

This is a fun variation for the kids on soccer scrimmages. It encourages lots of shots, so make sure your players know you want to see "shots, shots, shots." Shoot every time opportunity arises, but also set up shots with passes and movement without the ball to get open for passes and shots.

IV. Large Group Activity

A. <u>3 vs. 3 Scrimmage.</u>

Always emphasize position responsibilities and the concept of front and rear support for a teammate with the ball when playing 3 vs. 3. Today, however, make sure players know you want to see more shots than normal and that you want them to take more chances in shooting. Shoot long and from poor angles and even when defenders are in good position to block shot.

I. Warm Ups

A.   Confined Area Dribbling.

Emphasize "controlled dribbling" with lots of soft touches, changes of direction, keeping ball close to feet. Keep "eyes up" and constantly glance over shoulders behind you to see where all players are to avoid collisions. At first just have players dribble around area while you call out fast, slow, medium speeds and/or right or left turns, reverse, stop, etc. After a few minutes, stop drill and explain the four numbers and associated activity to the kids. They must concentrate so they "know what to do" when a number is called out. Smile and have fun during second half of drill.

B.   Scrimmage With Corner Goals.

Key to this game is keep it moving. Players can gain open routes to uncovered corner goals by making runs without the ball and calling for a long pass, etc. If players put forth full effort, this is an excellent conditioning drill also. Encourage use of full field and lots of cross passing to gain position advantage. You may want to limit touches to encourage more passing.

C.   Scrimmage--Man-to-Man.

This is a very physically demanding game if players really try. Tell them up front you will only go for 5 minutes, but you want everyone to try their hardest during the drill. Since the only player that can stop an opponent with the ball is the "opponent's man", there is a tendency in this drill for "long dribbling runs" every time the defender gets beat. The offensive player knows he has a "free run to the goal," especially if his "man" makes no attempt to recover after being beaten. Make sure the players know you expect them to "never quit" and to make every effort to recover goal-side position on their man once they have lost it. Remind them that a defensive player without the ball can often run faster than the offensive player who is dribbling a ball. Lastly, on a ball turnover to the opponents, players are <u>often not in good defensive position</u> at the moment of the turnover. A quick transition to defense is necessary to avoid hopelessly losing goal-side position on your man.

II. Individual Skill Activity
(Theme: Passing)

A.&B.   Straight-on Two-Touch Passing and Criss-Cross Two-Touch Passing.

The drills in IIA and IIB are really a progression using the same basic drill in different configurations. Key to both drills is to be sure players focus on making accurate passes with good touch and on making a perfect first touch to bring ball under control on the reception. The criss-cross drill is designed to challenge the concentration of the players by creating distractions to overcome.

C.   Pairs Passing on the Run.

Keys to this drill are (1) "leading" your receiver with the pass (i.e., pass to where the receiver will be when the ball gets to him, not where he is when the pass is made) and (2) receiving the ball with the "inside of the outside foot" making sure the ball does not get past the receiver.

D.   Two-Man Weave Inside a Lane.

This is a difficult drill for very young players. Let them work at it awhile without too much coaching. Just be sure the players switch sides by running behind their partner (staying inside the lane of cones) after every pass and that they then try to provide "front support" for a return pass.

III. Small Group Activity
None

IV. Large Group Activity

A.   3 vs. 3 Scrimmage.

Only difference today in playing this game is one backwards pass to a rear support player is required before a goal can be scored on any attack. Re-emphasize the importance of staying 10 yds. apart and knowing the responsibilities of each position and for providing front and rear support on offense and maintaining goal-side position on defense.

Warm Ups

A. **Numbers Game.**

Just let the kids have fun. Do no coaching although the game is excellent for developing tackling skills and aggressiveness.

B. **One-Step Tackle Practice.**

Emphasize the importance of making a proper first step with the non-kicking foot. It needs to be placed very close to the ball to gain full power and leverage advantage over the opponent. This drill has an obvious secondary purpose of developing aggressiveness for tackling.

C. **Jog Around Outside of Field.**

Stay in formation. No one quits running until time has elapsed or full distance has been run.

Individual Skill Activity
(Theme: Tackling)

A, B&C. **1 on 1 Tackling Inside a Lane, First Variation, and Second Variation.**

The progressive nature of Drills IIA, B and C is very important in teaching good tackling skills. They are designed to emphasize the importance of establishing and maintaining "goal-side position" to prevent shots and that goal-side position is a pre-requisite to making a good tackle of the ball.

In Drill IIA emphasize the three stages of tackling when a player with the ball is coming straight at you. (1) **Engage** opponent as far away from goal as possible, but have plenty of room between you and opponent (e.g., 5 to 10 yd. gap) to have time to react to his moves and maintain goal-side position. (2) **Close gap** between you and opponent by giving ground (i.e., moving backwards and sideways, always maintaining goal-side position) at a slower pace than opponent is advancing toward you. Never step forward to close gap until you are "touch-tight" to the opponent or have shoulder-to-shoulder contact. (3) **Make tackle** from goal-side position after letting gap close to touch-tight distance.

As you progress through Drills IIB and C the players will simply be trying to execute the same principals from increasingly difficult or challenging positions. In Drill IIB it may be necessary for the defender to use shoulder-to-shoulder force to gain goal-side position cutting off the offensive player and forcing him out of the side of the lane of cones. In Drill IIC, it may be necessary for the defender to use a slide tackle if he cannot gain goal-side position or sufficient shoulder-to-shoulder contact before the opponent reaches the shooting line.

III. Small Group Activity

A. **2 vs. 1 Scrimmage.**

Using a narrow grid and a 2 on 1 advantage, the team with 2 players should have many opportunities for "tackling." Emphasize maintaining goal-side position by each team and use of sound tackling techniques that have been practiced in the drills earlier today.

IV. Large Group Activity

A. **Full Team Scrimmage.**

Today do not limit to 3-sided teams unless you only have 6 players. The more players and congestion, the better for tackling opportunities during the scrimmage. No coaching today during the scrimmage except be sure teams use throw-ins and goal and corner kicks when appropriate. Complement good "goal-side position play" and "tackling" when opportunity arises.

I. Warm Ups

A. <u>**Jog Around Outside of Field.**</u>

Stay in formation. Push your teammates for a quicker pace than normal for 3 minutes. No one quits running until it is over.

B. <u>**In-Your-Face Drill--1 vs. 1 vs. 1 Shooting.**</u>

This is a great drill which will test the aggressiveness and leadership qualities of your players as well as develop their dribbling and shooting skills. Demand full effort by all players and total commitment by each player to score more goals than the other two players. Keep balls coming in quickly until all 7 have been used and call-out the score often. Try to match players of equal ability and aggressiveness, but mix them up a little also. Have championship playoffs.

II. Individual Skill Activities
(Theme: General Skills)

A. <u>**Multi-Skill Drill--One-Touch Shot.**</u>

Keep this drill moving quickly so players will have to jog or run into their next position and run balls back after retrieving. On the other hand, demand use of proper technique in throw-in, use of an instep (shoelaces) kick on the 1-touch shot using the proper foot each time.

<u>Special Note</u>: During Drills IIA and B the coach will actually be demonstrating for the players proper chest, thigh and foot receptions off the players' throw-in and proper set up passes for the shooters even though the players are not aware of this. It is important for the coach to use good technique during the early drills using a 2-touch reception and pass so that during Drill IIC below the players will be ready to act as servers.

B. <u>**Multi-Skill Drill--Two-Touch Shot.**</u>

Before starting this drill, pause for a moment to emphasize the importance of using a "perfect first touch" to set up a powerful accurate shot" whenever a player has time to do so. Explain that Drill IIA which they just finished , was intended for practicing situations when the player does not have sufficient time to use 2 touches but that it is always desirable to use 2 touches if you have the time because you will normally take a better shot.

C. <u>**Multi-Skill Drill--Players Act as Servers.**</u>

This drill is exactly the same as IIB above except when acting in the role of server the players get the opportunity to practice chest receptions, thigh receptions and foot receptions on the throw-ins from the shooters. The servers must use 2 touches to receive and execute an easy set-up pass for the shooters.

III. Small Group Activity

A. <u>**Zone Scrimmage--3 vs. 3.**</u>

This game is designed to encourage passing to the wings and use of the full width of the field to keep the defense spread out. Discourage dribbling by limiting number of touches to 3 or 4 by each player.

IV. Large Group Activity

A. **3 vs. 3 Scrimmage.**

The purpose of going to a regular 3 vs. 3 scrimmage after the zone scrimmage in IIIA above, is to remove the playing restrictions on the players and to let them have fun. Hopefully, they will continue to stay in their zones voluntarily after removing the cones that mark the zones.

I. Warm Ups

A. **Change Direction Running.**

Full speed running and immediate stops and changes of direction are keys to this drill. This drill is for agility and physical conditioning.

B. **Reverse Direction Dribbling.**

Reversing directions while dribbling is an invaluable skill in soccer. When you have plenty of time and when there are no defenders in the area, of course, reversing direction is easy and requires little skill. This drill, however, is designed to teach players how to come to a quick stop, control the ball and explode away from a threatening defender in the opposite direction.

Keys are as follows:

1. Keep ball close to feet when approaching defender.

2. Turn back toward defender and place body between defender and ball.

3. Step over ball with the foot that is closest to the defender and stop ball with inside of this foot.

4. Push ball 4 to 6 feet backwards (using the same foot) in the direction you want to go.

5. Explode with a burst of speed to catch up to ball and to run away from defender.

Pretending the "cones" are defenders in the drill, practice these steps reversing direction at each cone. Do it at slow to medium speed today as players learn the technique.

C. **Kicking Technique Practice--Stationary Ball.**

This drill is intended as a quick review of kicking techniques. Watch for the following:

1. Step with non-kicking foot.

2. Plant non-kicking foot 6 to 9 inches directly beside ball.

3. Non-kicking foot pointed directly at target.

4. Proper foot position for types of kick being used (e.g., shoelaces for instep, inside of foot, etc.).

5. Eyes on ball during kick.

6. Appropriate follow-through for type of kick being used.

D. **Kicking Technique Practice--Moving Ball.**

This drill is also intended as a quick review and practice session for proper kicking technique, but using a moving ball. Watch for same keys listed in IC above but watch carefully for "eyes on the ball.".

II. Individual Skill Activities
(Theme: Passing)

A. **Find Target Before Ball Arrives.**

This drill is again designed to practice passing with proper kicking technique but focuses on the skill of using your eyes to find your target before the ball arrives. As the reception and follow-up pass are made, the player's eyes must be focused on the ball. Insist on seeing your players use their eyes to both "find the receiver" and to "kick the ball."

First and Second Variations. These variations add the challenge of making an instantaneous decision on who to pass to, (i.e, finding the open man), while using proper kicking technique and executing good passes. To make these drills more fun score points for good passes and/or good decisions and compare to points given for successful defense.

III. Small Group Activity
None

IV. Large Group Activity

A.   **3 vs. 3 Scrimmage.**
Let 'em play! Use throw-ins and goal and corner kicks.

I. Warm Ups

A. **Team Keep Away.**

Give the winners a "butts-up penalty shot" at the losers (from 15 to 20 yds.) as a fun incentive to play hard. Encourage minimum 10 yd. distances between players and runs by teammates without the ball to provide front, rear and side support.

B. **3 vs. 3 Scrimmage.**

Scrimmage early today while the kids are fresh and minds are clear. Use the opportunity to emphasize playing positions and responsibilities again for rear and front support. Also remind them again on the rule of 10 yds. distance between players. Try also to encourage good tactics for all set plays on throw-ins, goal kicks and corner kicks.

II. Individual Skill Activities
(Theme: Ball Control)

A. **Ball Turnarounds.**

Getting a ball turned around and going the other direction when it is rolling away from the player is a surprisingly difficult task for young players. It is also a very important skill since quite often the ball is rolling uncontested straight toward your goal and there are opponents bearing down on it at the same time.

Most Common Error by Young Players. Young players will often run along side a rolling ball for many yards waiting for it to come to a stop so the player can run around it and make a good strong kick back up the field. During this drill, after one or more of your players have made this mistake, stop the drill and use the error as an opportunity to clearly show the kids that that technique is wrong and explain the key to proper technique.

Key to Proper Technique for Ball Turnarounds. The key to this skill is to get the players to kick the ball toward a sideline while running in the direction of their own goal, as soon as they catch up to the ball. The player can then turn his body in that direction on the run, chase the ball down, and start it back up the field the other direction. This is a far easier and quicker way for the player to turn the ball around than trying to run past the ball, turn around on a spot and be ready to kick the ball the opposite direction.

B. **Ball Turnarounds With Opponents.**

Players must be very aggressive and "win the race to the free ball." Using the techniques described above, the player trying to turn the ball around should kick the ball toward the sideline that is "away" from the other player or easiest for the kicker to get to first.

III. Small Group Activity

A. **Ball Control in Groups of 3.**

In the first phase of this drill, the key to turning the ball and passing it on to the player behind you is the "first touch." The first touch by the player in the middle must, of course, control the ball, but it must also allow the ball to pass by his body a few feet enabling him to turn around, to the side on which the ball arrives, taking one step "toward the person he is passing to" and make the pass. Of course, the second phase of this drill is intended to add the challenge of decision-making and communication under minimal pressure.

IV. Large Group Activity

A. Full Team Scrimmage.

The 3 vs. 3 scrimmage earlier has given the players the tactical training for the day. Just divide up the players and let them play and have fun. Tell them to be "cool, calm and collected" while controlling the ball. Be patient and make good decisions.

COMMENTARY

Session 16

I. Warm Ups

A. Team Keep Away.

Encourage perfect passes, perfect receptions and teamwork. Move without the ball to "support" your teammate with the ball. Tell your teammates "great play" when you see them "win the race for the free ball" and intercept a pass. Winners get a butts-up penalty shot on losers.

B. Dribble Around Outside of Field.

Do not make this a race, but be sure everyone is jogging or running slowly the entire time or distance.

C. Four-Sided Shooting Game.

Try to divide your most aggressive players evenly over the two teams. Encourage quick shooting and give players lots of opportunities for header goals when you throw-in new balls. Keep competitive atmosphere by calling out score and by keeping the score close by throwing balls in for easy scores by team that is behind.

II. Individual Skill Activities
(Theme: Set Play Tactics)

A. Throw-In Practice--Pairs.

Players must make full speed runs past the thrower to create the game condition tactics. Pace must be quick by all pairs and all pairs must keep up with group in front of them. Send best players off first.

B. Throw-In Tactics--Rear and Front Support.

Player A has "front support" for throw-in from player B and "rear support" from player C. Regardless of who player A throws the ball to, the receiver immediately needs front and side support from the other 2 players. Both plays invoke the same simple concept of providing front and rear (or side) support for the receiver of the throw-in immediately after the throw-in. Therefore, the support players (i.e., the 2 players without the ball) must make immediate movements without the ball to appropriate support positions.

III. Small Group Activity
None

IV. Large Group Activity

A. 3 vs. 3 Scrimmage.

Today emphasize proper tactics for set plays (e.g., throw-ins, goal and corner kicks) during the scrimmage. Stop play to be sure players are in proper positions for all set plays and that they are aware of the need to provide "support" for their teammate with the ball immediately upon restarting the game.

I. Warm Ups

A. **Brazilian Jog.**

Made famous by the Brazilian National Soccer Team. Use your creativity to come up with any type of "calls" you want. Main value of drill is aerobic so keep them running for the full time period. The "calls" are just for fun.

B. **1 vs. 1 Dribbling and Shooting.**

Offensive players practice their dribbling, fakes and shooting. Defensive players should be disciplined about using the 3 phases of tackling:

1. ***"Engage" Opponent.*** Defender sprints fast to engage opponent as far away from goal as possible, but leaving a 5 to 10 yd. gap or cushion between him and opponent.

2. ***"Close" On Opponent.*** By giving ground slower than opponent is advancing, but always maintaining goal-side position, let the gap between players close by the time offensive player reaches penalty box (i.e., shooting range).

3. ***Tackle Ball.*** When defender is "touch-tight" to opponent (i.e., "closed on opponent") or has established shoulder-to-shoulder contact, defender tackles ball and moves it toward sideline and then up the field.

II. Individual Skill Activity
(Theme: Decision-Making)

A. **Read the Defender Drill.**

When first running this drill instruct the defender, C, to run straight at player A. In this situation A should decide to pass to B since B should be open. A, however, should be calm and cool and make a good collection and reception of the ball and then make a perfect pass to B. A should be instructed to not panic because of the pressure from C.

After a few minutes, instruct the C players to move on a diagonal line to cover player B. In this case, A should decide to "fake" a pass to B and dribble past C for a shot. After a few more minutes, let C defend by instinct and let A read the defender and make his decision to pass or dribble. A will likely have to make a few feints to cause C to commit to a defensive position making A's decision more clear (i.e., A may have to initiate a dribble move forward forcing C to move to defend him, but then stop and pass to B).

B. **Water Break.**

C. **2 vs. 1 Dribbling and Shooting.**

Defenders practice same techniques discussed in IB above. Offensive players now attack in pairs and should attempt to use wall pass tactics, or spread wide tactics to gain offensive advantages on the single defender.

III. Small Group Activity
None

IV. Large Group Activity

A. Full Team Scrimmage.

Prior to scrimmage remind players that today's drills were intended to help them stay calm and to make good decisions while playing soccer under pressure. Give points during the scrimmage for good decision-making and cool play.

I. Warm Ups

A. **Dribbling Jingle Jangle Races.**

Just have fun racing.

B. **Ball Touch Drill.**

Call for quick feet. See who is faster than the "road runner" cartoon character.

C. **3 vs. 3 vs. 3 Scrimmage.**

This drill will be a challenge for players of this age to understand. At first, stay near the mid-field line to help players stay on proper end of field and to help them play the game properly. Call score out loud to encourage competition and be sure players on each team stay a minimum 10 yds. apart. Defense should dominate this drill.

II. Individual Skill Activities
(Theme: Defense)

A. **Progressive Defensive Tactics Drill.**

This drill is designed to emphasize the importance of good defensive position (i.e., "goal-side position" between opponent and goal) in preventing shots, stopping penetration and being in a good position to tackle the ball. At the beginning of the drill, ask your players whether it is more important for a fullback to maintain "goal-side position" or to "tackle the ball." The answer should be "goal-side position" because we do not want to risk giving up shots near our goal. Use quick feet and short shuffle steps staying low to ground when attempting to maintain goal-side positions. Offensive players must use fakes and feints and many changes of speed and direction to try to get around defenders.

III. Small Group Activity
None

IV. Large Group Activity

A. **3 vs. 3 Scrimmage.**

During the scrimmage today give random points (goals) to each team whose players demonstrate excellent goal-side position on defense. Be a little stingy demanding excellent play for this extra point.

General Comment

Since this is your last week of practice, take extra care to create a light and fun atmosphere at practice this week. Be sure the kids end the season with lots of laughter, smiles and uninhibited fun during practice.

Minimize coaching except to explain the drills and to keep them running smoothly. Use fun nicknames for your kids such as bullet, enforcer, Darth Vadar, Luke Skywalker, Road Runner, etc.

I. Warm Ups

A. Pairs Passing.

Players should jog only at medium to slow speed while passing. Place emphasis on making it easy for your partners to receive and control the ball and keep running down field. Good accuracy and touch.

B. Cross, Control and Shoot.

Key coaching point: If you have the time, always bring ball under control with perfect first touch before shooting.

II. Individual Skill Activities
(Theme: Passing)

A. 3-Man Weave.

Let 'em run and have fun, but take pride in perfect passes and running hard around your teammates and back toward the middle.

B. Water Break.

C. Wall Pass Drill.

Key to this drill is the "1-touch" return pass to A from players B, C and D. These players must use an "inside of foot" pass and make the pass very soft and controlled for A to pick back up easily. Key coaching phrase "make it easy for A to receive the wall pass."

III. Small Group Activity

A. Zone Scrimmage 3 vs. 3.

This game is designed to encourage passing to the wings and use of the full width of the field to keep the defense spread out. Discourage dribbling by limiting the number of touches to 3 or 4 per player.

IV. Large Group Activity

A. Running Relay Races.

Just for fun. Laugh and smile with the kids.

General Comment

Today practice has been designed for a light fun workout with some fun competition. The kids are familiar with all the drills so they should be easy to run.

Be sure this last practice is fun for the kids and dole out the compliments to every player. Point out every good play you see.

I. Warm Ups

A. **Confined Area Dribbling.**

Coach can make this fun by a few rapid fire changes of direction and speed, quick stops, etc.

B. **Confined Area Passing.**

Use fun nicknames for the kids as they pass the ball around, such as "Elway to Jackson," "Bird to McHale," "Donald Duck to Pluto," etc.

C. **Scatter Game.**

The "10 second count down" for the last 2 players will add some fun.

D. **Team Keep Away.**

Before starting, be sure teams are aware of the reward for the winners of a butts-up penalty shot at the losers and make losers take a short penalty run to their water bottles.

II. Individual Skill Activity
(Theme: All Skills)

A. **1 vs. 1 Scrimmage.**

Keep the games moving with new balls, etc., and the players running hard for each 2-minute period. To make it more fun, have one blue and one red jerseyed player in each pair and combine the scores of each 1 vs. 1 scrimmage by red and blue. That way the players playing goalie will cheer for their teammate and play harder.

III. Small Group Activity
None

IV. Large Group Activity

A. **3 vs. 3 Scrimmage.**

Just let them have fun. Minimize coaching and give out the compliments.

B. **Team Discussion.**

Take this 5-minute opportunity to put soccer in proper perspective in the "Big Picture of Life." Explain that what the kids have "really" done in soccer this year is:

1. Have fun and make God proud of them by trying hard and using the talents and abilities God gave them to play soccer to the very best of their ability.

2. To help one another be better players and to sacrifice their individual goals for the good of the "team."

3. To build life lasting friendships with their teammates and coaches.

These accomplishments are far more important than the won-loss record of the team.